D0462742

Rath & Strong's

Six Sigma
Advanced Tools
Pocket Guide

Augustine A. Stagliano

McGraw-Hill

New York Chicago San Francisco Lisbon London
Madrid Mexico City Milan New Delhi San Juan
Seoul Singapore Sydney Toronto

This publication is designed to provide accurate and authoritative information in regard to the subject matter covered. It is sold with the understanding that neither the author nor the publisher is engaged in rendering legal, accounting, or other professional service. If legal advice or other expert assistance is required, the services of a competent professional person should be sought.

—*From a Declaration of Principles jointly
adopted by a Committee of the American Bar
Association and a Committee of Publishers*

McGraw-Hill books are available at special quantity discounts to use as premiums and sales promotions, or for use in corporate training programs. For more information, please write to the Director of Special Sales, McGraw-Hill, 2 Penn Plaza, New York, NY 10121-2298. Or contact your local bookstore.

This book is printed on recycled, acid-free paper containing a minimum of 50% recycled de-inked fiber.

CONTENTS

INTRODUCTION

As a Six Sigma practitioner with over 10 years in the game, I recall how my colleagues and I yearned for a handy reference that could help us to effectively apply the statistical tools that we were introduced to in our Six Sigma training. Many Six Sigma books are now available. Some are essentially statistics textbooks with a Six Sigma slant, and others just don't have enough horsepower to satisfy the needs of many practicing Green Belts and Black Belts. This book fills that void and provides Six Sigma professionals with a practical guide on the use of advanced tools, such as analysis of variance, multiple regression, and design of experiments. This book is not intended to be a textbook. It is geared toward those individuals who have been or will be trained at the Green Belt or Black Belt level, providing the user with a practical reference for the application of Six Sigma tools.

I hope that you enjoy using this book as much as I enjoyed writing it for you.

—Augustine A. Stagliano

CHAPTER 1
Tool Selection Guide

The purpose of this chapter and the charts on the inside covers is to provide guidance on the selection of the most appropriate tools for your Six Sigma project.

Most of the examples presented in the *Pocket Guide* use *Microsoft Excel* or *Minitab* statistical software. Table 1-1 provides references to *Minitab* commands, along with the chapters and page numbers for specific examples found in the *Pocket Guide*. Table 1-2 lists the *Microsoft Excel* built-in statistical functions that are used in some of the examples in the book.

An an example of how to use these tables, suppose we're interested in comparing the average performance levels before and after the implementation of a process improvement, i.e., a test of sample means for two groups. Referring to the reference tables on the inside covers, we have a choice of either the Two Sample Z-Test or Two Sample t-Test. Next, we would refer to the chapter and pages associated with those tools to identify the best one to use. For our example, we refer to Chapter 5, page 65 for the Two Sample Z-Test and page 72 for the Two Sample t-Test. Next, we refer to Tables 1-1 and 1-2 to determine the relevant *Minitab* commands or *Excel* function to use. If we don't know what the standard deviation is, we select the Two Sample t-test. Otherwise, we use the Two Sample Z-test.

If we decide to use a Two-Sample t-test, Table 1-1 provides us with the sequence of *Minitab* toolbar commands that will allow us to perform that test:

Stat → Basic Statistics → 2-Sample t

Table 1-1 also refers us to specific examples in the *Pocket Guide* that we can review to brush-up on specific techniques, as we see fit.

Table 1-2 provides the sequence of commands for the *Excel* statistical functions that are used in this book.

MINITAB COMMANDS

Statistical Tool	Minitab Commands	Chap	Page
Probability Plots and Data Transformations			
Probability Plots	Graph/Probability Plot	2	23
Box-Cox Transform	Stat/Control Charts/Box-Cox Transformation	2	30
Hypothesis Testing			
Z-Test	Stat/Basic Statistics/ 1-Sample Z	5	63
t-Test	Stat/Basic Statistics/ 1-Sample t	5	69
Two-Sample t-Test	Stat/Basic Statistics/ 2-Sample t	5	73, 74
Paired t-Test	Stat/Basic Statistics/ Paired t	5	76, 77
Two-Sample Proportion Test	Stat/Basic Statistics/ 2 Proportions	5	80, 81
Correlation & Regression Analysis			
Scatter Plot	Graph/Scatter Plot	7	117
Correlation Matrix	Stat/Basic Statistics/ Correlation	7	120, 122
Regression Analysis	Stat/Regression/ Regression	8	127, 133 136, 142 152, 153

Table 1-1. (continued on pages 4-6)

MINITAB COMMANDS

Statistical Tool	Minitab Commands	Chap	Page
Control Charts			
p Chart	Stat/Control Charts/ Attribute Charts/P	6	96
np Chart	Stat/Control Charts/ Attribute Charts/NP	6	99
c Chart	Stat/Control Charts/ Attribute Charts/C	6	100
u Chart	Stat/Control Charts/ Attribute Charts/U	6	103
Individuals Chart	Stat/Control Charts/ Variables Chars for Individuals/Individuals	6	105
Moving Range (MR) Chart	Stat/Control Charts/ Variables Chars for Individuals/Moving Range	6	106
Range (R) Chart	Stat/Control Charts/ Variables Chars for Subgroups/R	6	108
$\bar{x}$ Chart	Stat/Control Charts/ Variables Chars for Subgroups/Xbar	6	109
EWMA Chart	Stat/Control Charts/ Time Weighted Charts/ EWMA	6	112

Table 1-1. (continued)

MINITAB COMMANDS

Statistical Tool	Minitab Commands	Chap	Page
Design of Experiments (DOE)			
Factorial Design Matrices	Stat/DOE/Factorial/ Create Factorial Design	9	163, 165 175, 176 181-187
Factorial Design Analysis	Stat/DOE/Factorial/ Analyze Factorial Design	9	164, 172 175, 187
Factorial Plots	Stat/DOE/Factorial/ Factorial Plots	9	170, 171
Analysis of Variance (ANOVA)			
One Way ANOVA	Stat/ANOVA/One Way	10	193
Two Way ANOVA	Stat/ANOVA/Two Way	10	195, 197
Nested ANOVA	Stat/ANOVA/Fully Nested ANOVA	10	201
Analysis of Means (ANOM)	Stat/ANOVA/Analysis of Means	10	204
Main Effects Plot	Stat/ANOVA/Main Effects Plot	10	206
Interaction Plot	Stat/ANOVA/Interaction Plot	10	208

Table 1-1. (continued)

MINITAB COMMANDS

Statistical Tool	Minitab Commands	Chap	Page
Analysis of Variance (ANOVA)			
Interval Plot	Stat/ANOVA/Interval Plot	10	210
Balanced ANOVA	Stat/ANOVA/Balanced ANOVA	10	211
General Linear Models (GLM)	Stat/ANOVA/General Linear Model	10	213

Table 1-1. (continued)

EXCEL STATISTICAL FUNCTIONS

Excel Function	Chapter	Page
BINOMDIST(x, n, p, c)		
x = # of successes n = # of trials (sample sheet) p = probability of success c = TRUE for cumulative probability c = FALSE for individual probability	2	11, 12
POISSON(x, λ, c)		
x = # of events λ = mean c = TRUE for cumulative probability c = FALSE for individual probability	2	13
NORMDIST(x, μ, σ, c)		
x = variable of interst λ = mean σ = standard deviation c = TRUE for cumulative probability	2	16, 17
EXPONDIST(x, m, c)		
x = variable of interst μ = mean $(1 \div \lambda)$ c = TRUE for cumulative probability	2	19
WEIBULL(x, β, δ, c)		
x = variable of interst β = shape δ = scale parameter c = TRUE for cumulative probability	2	21

Table 1-2. (continued on page 8)

EXCEL STATISTICAL FUNCTIONS

Excel Function	Chapter	Page
CONFIDENCE(α, σ, n,)		
α = alpha value = (i – desired confidence) σ = standard deviation n = sample size	4	50
TINV(p, df)		
p = probability (two-tailed t-distribution) df = degrees of freedom = $(n - 1)$	4	51
NORMSIN(p)		
p = probability (normal distribution)	4	52
CHINV(p, df)		
p = probability (chi-squared distribution) df = degrees of freedom = $(n - 1)$	4	53

Table 1-2. (continued)

CHAPTER TWO
Probability Distributions

What Is a Probability Distribution?

A probability distribution is a mathematical model that is used to describe the characteristics (shape, center, and spread) of a population. Many different types of distributions exist; each one used to determine the probability of occurrence for a specific value or range of values contained within a population.

Application of Probability Distributions in Six Sigma

In Six Sigma, probability distributions have a wide variety of applications and form the foundation of many statistical methods and tests. Examples of applications are: performance baselining, process monitoring and control, comparison of multiple processes, predicting the occurrence of future events, etc.

Discrete Probability Distributions

Variables represented by a discrete distribution (Figure 2-1) are integers, either binomial (0 or 1, yes or no, etc.) or counts (number of days, number of defective items, etc.). The x-axis is the variable of interest and the y-axis is the corresponding probability of occurrence for that variable.

An example of a discrete x-variable is "type of defect" and the y-variable is the likelihood that each of the defect types will occur.

DISCRETE DISTRIBUTION

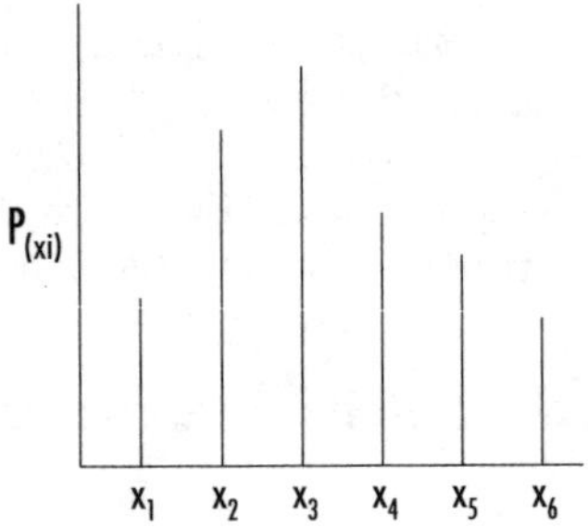

Figure 2-1.

BINOMIAL DISTRIBUTION

The binomial distribution (Figure 2-2) is used in settings where items are evaluated using attributes, such as in quality control settings where the proportion of defective product is evaluated.

BINOMIAL DISTRIBUTION

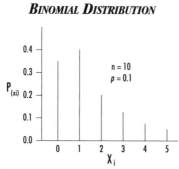

Figure 2-2.

The probability function for the binomial distribution is:

$$P_{(x)} = \binom{n}{x} p^x (1-p)^{n-x}$$

where:

$P_{(x)}$ is the probability of exactly "x" successes

p is the probability of success

x is the number of successes

n is the number of trials

$x = 0, 1, 2, 3, \ldots, n$

mean $= np$

variance $= np\,(1\text{-}p)$

Example 1. Using Excel, calculate the probability of exactly 30 defective items occurring in a production run of 500 items, given a population defect rate of 5%.

BINOMDIST(30, 500, .05, false)

$P_{(x=30)} = 0.046$

The probability of producing exactly 30 defective items in a production run of 500 items is 0.046 (4.6%).

Example 2. Using Excel, calculate the probability of 30 or fewer defective units occurring in a production run of 500 units, given a population defect rate of 5%.

BINOMDIST(30, 500, .05, true)

$P(x \le 30) = 0.869$

The probability of producing 30 or fewer defective items is 0.869 (86.9%).

POISSON DISTRIBUTION

The Poisson distribution (Figure 2.3) is used when it is desired to determine the probability of the number of occurrences on a per-unit basis (per-unit time, per-unit area, per-unit volume, etc.). Typical applications are in quality control settings where it is desired to measure defects-per-unit. The Poisson distribution may be used to approximate the binomial distribution when n is large and $p < 0.1$.

The probability function for the Poisson distribution is:

$$P_{(x)} = \frac{e^{-\lambda} \lambda^x}{x!}$$

where:

e is the base of the natural logarithm = 2.718.

x is the number of occurrences per unit

$x = 0, 1, 2, 3, \dots, n$

mean = λ

variance = λ

POISSON DISTRIBUTION

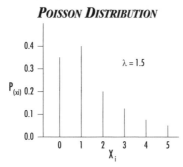

Figure 2-3.

Example 1. Using Excel, calculate the probability of exactly 5 pinhole defects occurring in a square meter of aluminum foil, given an average defects-per-unit of 3.

POISSON(5, 3, false)

$P_{(x=5)} = 0.101$

The probability of exactly 5 defects-per-unit is 0.101 (10.1%).

Example 2. Using Excel, calculate the probability of 5 or fewer pinhole defects occurring in a square meter of aluminum foil, given an average defects-per-unit of 3.
POISSON(5, 3, true)

$P_{(x \le 5)} = 0.916$.

The probability of 5 or fewer defects-per-unit is 0.916 (91.6%).

Continuous Probability Distributions

Values in a continuous distribution are measured on a continuous scale (Figure 2-4). Examples of continuous variables are: length, temperature, volume, etc.

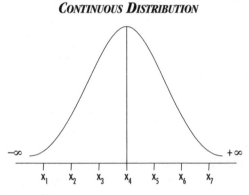

CONTINUOUS DISTRIBUTION

Figure 2-4.

NORMAL DISTRIBUTION

The normal distribution is both the most important and most commonly applied probability distribution in Six Sigma. Figure 2.5 is an example of a normal distribution model of the time required to process and deliver a customer order.

The normal distribution is often referred to as a "normal curve" and has the following characteristics:

1. smooth and continuous

2. bell shaped and symmetrical
3. both tails are asymptotic to the x-axis
4. the total area under the distribution curve equals 1
5. the mean, median, and mode have the same value

The probability function for the normal distribution is:

$$f_{(x)} = \frac{1}{\sigma\sqrt{2\pi}}e^{-\frac{1}{2}\left(\frac{x-\mu}{\sigma}\right)^2}$$

where:

e is the base of the natural logarithm = 2.718

$\pi = 3.142$

x is the variable of interest

$-\infty \leq x \leq +\infty$

mean = μ

variance = σ^2

NORMAL DISTRIBUTION

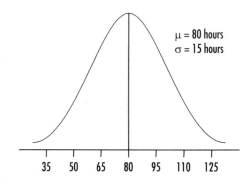

$\mu = 80$ hours
$\sigma = 15$ hours

35   50   65   80   95   110   125

Figure 2-5.

Because of its special characteristic of symmetry, it is convenient to visualize the normal distribution as being divided into units of standard deviation (referred to as z-values). Figure 2-6 illustrates how z-values correspond to actual measurements, using Figure 2-5 as the basis of comparison.

ORIGINAL UNITS OF MEASURE AND THEIR CORRESPONDING Z-VALUES

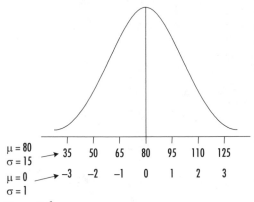

$\mu = 80$	$\rightarrow$ 35	50	65	80	95	110	125
$\sigma = 15$							
$\mu = 0$	$\rightarrow$ −3	−2	−1	0	1	2	3
$\sigma = 1$							

Figure 2-6.

he formula for converting actual values into z-values is:

$$Z = \frac{X - \mu}{\sigma}$$

Example 1. Calculate the z-value for x = 95 hours, given a process that has a normal distribution, with $\mu = 80$ hours and $\sigma = 15$ hours.

$$Z = \frac{95 - 80}{15} = 1$$

A normal distribution where $\mu = 0$ and $\sigma = 1$ is called a *standard normal* or *z distribution*. It is important to note that the area under the normal curve is distributed as follows:

$-1 < z < +1 = 68.3\%$ of the total area
$-2 < z < +2 = 95.4\%$ of the total area
$-3 < z < +3 = 99.7\%$ of the total area

Example 2. Using Excel, calculate the probability of $x < 85$ hours occurring in a assembly process with a mean of 100 hours and standard deviation of 15.2 hours (x is the time required to assemble a diesel engine).

NORMDIST(85, 100, 15.2, true)

$P(x < 85) = 0.162$

The probability of assembling a diesel engine in less than 85 hours is 0.162 (16.2%).

Example 3. Using Excel, calculate the probability of assembling a diesel engine within 85 hours to 125 hours.

NORMDIST(125, 100, 15.2, true)

$P_{(x < 125)} = 0.950$

$P_{(85 < x < 125)} = P(x < 125) - P_{(x < 85)}$

$P_{(85 < x < 125)} = 0.950 - 0.162 = 0.788$

The probability of assembling a diesel engine within 85 hours to 125 hours is 0.788 (78.8%).

EXPONENTIAL DISTRIBUTION

The exponential distribution (Figure 2.7) is used when it is desired to determine the probability of an event occurring over space or time intervals. Typical applications are in reliability engineering (product life expectancy) and in customer service settings (waiting time at a supermarket checkout or bank). The mean of an exponential distribution is often referred to as mean time to failure, but can also be thought of as mean time to service in customer service applications.

EXPONENTIAL DISTRIBUTION

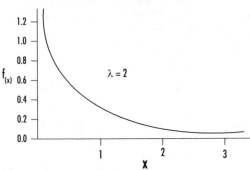

Figure 2-7.

The probability function for the exponential distribution is:

$$f_{(x)} = \lambda e^{-\lambda x}$$

where:

λ is the failure rate or service rate

e is the base of the natural logarithm = 2.718
x is the random variable ($x \geq 0$)

$$\text{mean} = \frac{1}{\lambda}$$

$$\text{variance} = \frac{1}{\lambda^2}$$

Example 1. Using Excel, calculate the probability of an engine bearing failing within 350 hours, given a typical service life of 500 hours.

Note: you must calculate average time to failure first $(1/\lambda)$: $1/500 = 0.002$

EXPONDIST(350, 0.002, true)

$P_{(x < 350)} = 0.503$

The probability of a bearing failing within 350 hours is 0.503 (50.3%).

Example 2. Using Excel, calculate the probability of an engine bearing failing after 500 hours of service.

EXPONDIST(500, 0.002, true)

$P_{(x < 500)} = 0.632$

$P_{(x > 500)} = 1 - P(x < 500)$

$P_{(x > 500)} = 1 - 0.632 = 0.368$

The probability of an engine bearing remaining in service for more than 500 hours is 0.368 (36.8%).

WEIBULL DISTRIBUTION

The Weibull distribution is a very flexible family of distributions; its shape is determined by the values used for β, δ, and γ (Figure 2-8). The Weibull distribution is equivalent to the exponential distribution (mean = $1/\delta$) when γ is zero and β is 1. Typical applications are in reliability modeling of time to failure for electronic, structural, and mechanical systems.

WEIBULL DISTRIBUTION

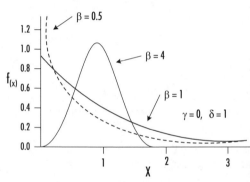

Figure 2-8.

The probability function for the Weibull distribution is:

$$f_{(x)} = \frac{\beta}{\delta} \left(\frac{x - \gamma}{\delta} \right)^{\beta-1} e^{-\left(\frac{x-\gamma}{\delta} \right)^{\beta}}$$

where:
β is shape parameter ($\beta > 0$), which defines the shape of the distribution

is the scale parameter ($\delta > 0$), which is the magnitude of the x-axis

is the location parameter ($-\infty < \gamma < +\infty$), which determines the location of the distribution relative to the x-axis

is the base of the natural logarithm $= 2.718$

is the random variable of interest ($x \geq \gamma$)

$$\text{mean} = \gamma + \delta\Gamma\left(1 + \frac{1}{\beta}\right)$$

$$\text{variance} = \delta^2\left[\Gamma\left(1 + \frac{2}{\beta}\right) - \Gamma\left(1 + \frac{1}{\beta}\right)^2\right]$$

Example 1. The Weibull distribution is used to model the failure distribution of an integrated circuit, using $\gamma = 0$, $\delta = 2,000$, and $\beta = 0.5$.

Using Excel, calculate the probability that the integrated circuits will have a life of less than 5,000 hours.

WEIBULL(5000, 0.5, 2000, true)

$P_{(x < 350)} = 0.794$

The probability of an integrated circuit failing within 5,000 hours is 0.794 (79.4%).

Example 2. Using Excel and the information from Example 1, what is the probability that an integrated circuit will last at least 8000 hours?

WEIBULL(8000, 0.5, 2000, true)

$P_{(x < 8000)} = 0.865$

$P_{(x > 8000)} = (1 - 0.865) = 0.135$

The probability of an integrated circuit lasting at least 8,000 hours is 0.135 (13.5%).

Probability Plots

Probability plots are used to determine how well our data fit a given probability distribution. Probability plots are powerful tools that we use to identify the distribution model that best fits our process.

Interpreting probability plots is easy. The plot consists of a centerline, with an outer band above and a lower band below it (Figure 2-9).

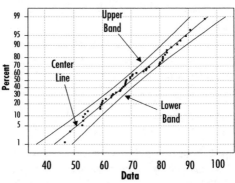

NORMAL PROBABILITY PLOT

Figure 2-9.

The closer the plotted points are lined-up to the center line, the better is the fit of the data to the probability distribution being evaluated. If all of the points lie within the

pper and lower bands, the probability model is a good fit
or your data.

xample: The life performance distribution for a specialty
amp is shown in Figure 2-10. Determine the probability
nodel that best fits this distribution.

LAMP LIFE PERFORMANCE

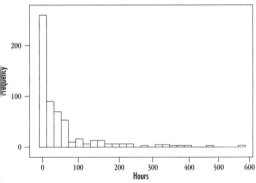

igure 2-10.

Let's compare the results using three different probability
lots: (1) normal, (2) exponential, and (3) weibull:

1. *Normal Probability Plot:* the extremely large deviation from
   the centerline indicates that this distribution isn't even
   remotely similar to a normal distribution (Figure 2-11, p.
   24). The vertical arrangement of data at the lower end of
   the plot shows that there are far more observations than
   should be expected. Similarly, the data at the high end of the

NORMAL PROBABILITY PLOT

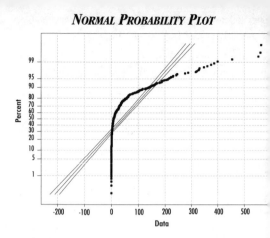

Figure 2-11.

plot shows the presence of extreme values; values that are much higher than would be expected (positively skewed).

2. *Exponential Probability Plot:* since there is a large deviation of the points from the centerline, the exponential distribution isn't the appropriate probability model (Figure 2-12, p. 25). The plot shows that there are more low values and fewer middle-to-high values than should be expected.

3. *Weibull Probability Plot:* the data is arranged tightly around the centerline from the 3rd percentile upward (Figure 2-13, p. 26). The fit below the 3rd percentile isn't as good, but should not be considered a problem.

The data fits the weibull probability distribution very well, making it the appropriate model to apply.

EXPONENTIAL PROBABILITY PLOT

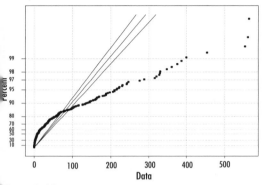

Figure 2-12.

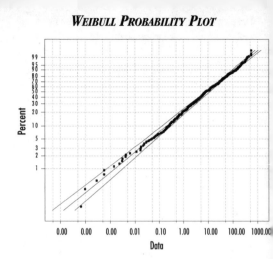

WEIBULL PROBABILITY PLOT

Figure 2-13.

Transforming Non-Normal Data to Normal

When it is desired to transform data for statistical procedures that are affected by non-normal data (e.g., linear regression, certain types of control charts, etc.), data transforms having differing degrees of strength can be applied. Some of the more useful transforms (lowest to highest strength) are:

- square root
- logarithm (e or $\log_{(10)}$)
- negative reciprocal

After transforming data, a probability plot should be generated to ensure that the transformation achieved the desired result.

Example: Transform the data represented in Figure 2-14 and use a probability plot to confirm the normality of the transformed data.

The original data was successfully transformed using a $Log_{(10)}$ transform (Figure 2-15), as confirmed by a normal probability plot of the transformed data (Figure 2-16), which shows only a slight deviation between the lower 1% to 5% of the data.

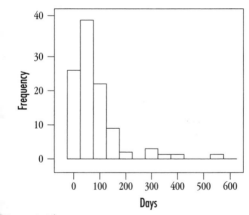

Figure 2-14.

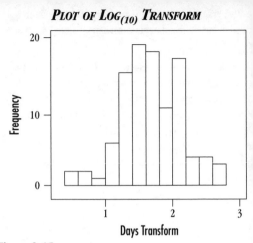

Figure 2-15.

NORMAL PROBABILITY PLOT
LOG(10) TRANSFORMED DATA

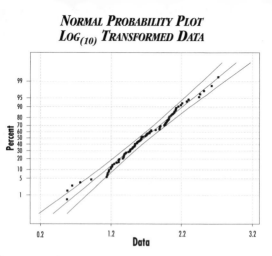

Figure 2-16.

BOX-COX TRANSFORMATION

The Box-Cox transformation consists of a family of transformations that are based on the following formula:

$$X_{(transform)} = X^\lambda$$

where:

$X_{(transform)}$ is the transformed variable

X is the variable being transformed

λ is the exponent of the variable being transformed

Note: when $\lambda = 0$, the natural log (e) is used as the transformation value.

The value used for λ determines the relative "strength" of the transformation. Table 2-1 shows the effect that different λ values have on the transformed value, using $X = 10$ as an example. Most statistical software packages can be used to easily generate an optimal λ for the Box-Cox transformation.

Example. This example illustrates the steps involved in applying the Box-Cox methodology. A histogram of the original data is shown in Figure 2-17.

TRANSFORMATION EXAMPLE

Lambda (λ)	Transform	Transform Value for $X = 10$
2	X^2	100
1	X^1	10
0.5	$X^{0.5}$	3.16
0	$Log_{(e)}X$	2.30
−1	$X^{-0.5}$	0.32
−0.5	X^{-1}	0.1
−2	X^{-2}	0.01

Table 2-1.

ORIGINAL DATA

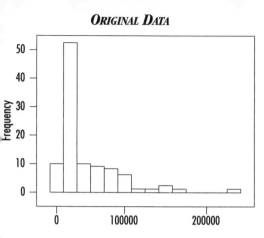

Figure 2-17.

First, a Box-Cox λ optimization was generated using *Minitab*. Figure 2-18 shows the optimal λ value, which corresponds to the minimum value of y, which is $\lambda = 0$.

Since $\lambda = 0$, $\log_{(e)}$ is used to transform the data. Figure 2-19 is a histogram of the transformed data.

Finally, a normal probability plot is generated (Figure 2-20) to determine if the transformation was successful. Since all of the points are contained within the bands, we can safely use the transformed data.

λ **Optimization**

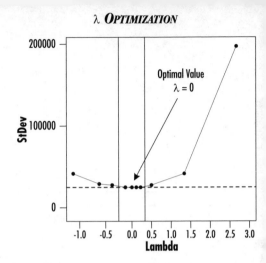

Figure 2-18.

TRANSFORMED DATA

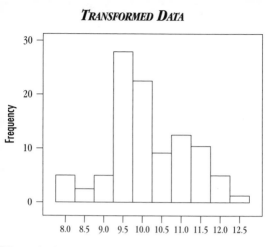

Figure 2-19.

NORMAL PROBABILITY PLOT
(TRANSFORMED DATA)

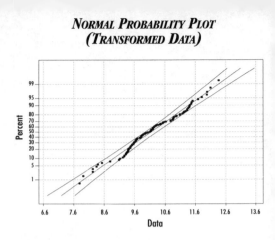

Figure 2-20.

How to Use Probability Distributions

1. Estimate sample size.
2. Select the appropriate model using the *Probability Distribution Matrix* (Table 2-2, pp. 35-36).
3. If using continuous data, use probability plots to determine the distribution model that works best with your data.
4. If it is desirable to convert your non-normal data to normal, apply the Box-Cox transformation.
5. When using transformed data, be sure to convert back to the original measurement scale before reporting results.

PROBABILITY DISTRIBUTION MATRIX

Data Type	Distribution	Application	Page
Discrete	Binomial	Determine the probability of occurrence of a discrete variable. Examples: number of defective units, late deliveries, late payments, injuries.	10
	Poisson	Determine the probability of occurrence of a discrete variable on a per-unit basis. Examples: number of defects-per-unit of an assembled product, number of mistakes-per-invoice, number of injuries-per-week	12
Continuous	Normal	Determine the probability of occurrence of a continuous variable. Examples: invoice processing cycle-time, inventory counts and valuation, physical measurements	19
	Exponential	Determine the probability of occurrence of a continuous variable over a space or time interval. Examples: product life expectancy, customer waiting time.	18

Table 2-2. (Continued on next page)

PROBABILITY DISTRIBUTION MATRIX

Data Type	Distribution	Application	Page
Continuous	Weibull	Determine the probability of occurrence of a continuous variable over a space or time interval. Examples: reliability of electronic, mechanical, and material systems.	20

Table 2-2. (Continued)

CHAPTER THREE
Sampling

Why Use Sampling?

We often need to develop an understanding of populations that are very large in size. However, due to time and cost constraints, it's usually impractical or impossible to work with an entire population. Statistical sampling allows us to gather useful population information without requiring a look at the entire population.

Application of Sampling in Six Sigma

In Six Sigma, sampling is applied in virtually all areas. Applications include hypothesis testing, probability distribution modeling, ANOVA, design of experiments, measurement system validation, and regression analysis. Sampling can be used to estimate population and process parameters (such as average, variation, and proportions) efficiently and economically.

One of the major benefits of using statistical sampling is our ability to specify the degree of accuracy and precision of our statistical test before we actually perform the test.

Sample Types

Samples are either *judgmental* or *statistical*. A *judgmental sample* is selected based upon the opinion of the analyst and the results may be used to make inferences only about those items from within the sample, i.e., the actual observations.

A *statistical sample* is randomly selected from the entire population and the results may be used to make inferences about the entire population. Table 3-1 illustrates the differences between these two approaches.

JUDGMENTAL VS. STATISTICAL SAMPLING

Judgmental Sample	Statistical Sample
Sample is selected based on knowledge and experience.	Sample is selected randomly.
Only a subset of the population is included in the selection process.	Entire population is included in the selection process.
Sample is *assumed* to be representative of the population.	Sample *is* representative of the population.

Table 3-1.

Sampling Terminology

Population—all of the items that make up the group you're interested in. Examples are: all gear suppliers, all gear suppliers located in the midwest, all gears used in car doors, etc The population should be precisely defined when you begin outlining your sampling plan.

Sampling Frame—a listing, database, or other specific identifier of all items that will be included in your sample, e.g., a shipment record listing all gears that comprise the population of interest.

Sampling Unit—the actual item that will be sampled, e.g., an individual gear.

Types of Population Data

Data is classified into two general categories: *attributes* and *variables*. When using *attributes* data, the focus is on learning about one or more specific non-numerical characteristics of the population being sampled. Examples of attributes are: red or green, yes or no, small or medium or large, etc. With *variables* data, an actual numerical estimate is derived for one or more characteristics of the population being sampled. Examples of variables are: diameter, length, number of days, etc.

What Affects Sample Size?

When working with *attributes* data, the key drivers of sample size are sample precision (how close the estimated value is to the actual population value) and the expected value of p (the population proportion used in the sample size calculation—refer to *Formula for Estimating Sample Size with Attributes Data*).

When working with *variables* data, sample precision and population variance have the greatest influence on sample size. Those populations having high variance require larger sample sizes than those having low variance for any given sample precision.

With both *attributes* and *variables* data, if greater degrees of sample precision are desired, larger sample sizes will be required.

Confidence

Confidence is the probability that the actual population value being estimated will be contained within the precision interval of our estimate. The precision interval represents the total amount of sampling error that you should expect for any specific sample size.

Figure 3-1 shows the relationship between sample size and precision for estimating the proportion of defects in a transactional process, using a confidence level of 95%. Sample sizes become larger as the precision interval becomes smaller (smaller precision intervals = better estimates).

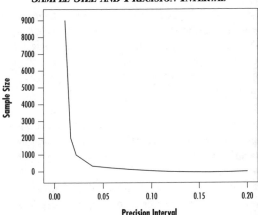

SAMPLE SIZE AND PRECISION INTERVAL

Figure 3-1.

Sampling Techniques

SIMPLE RANDOM SAMPLE

The sample is selected in a purely random fashion, i.e., every item in the population has an equal chance of being included in the sample. This is the most basic form of random sampling and the most generally applied in estimating population values.

STRATIFIED RANDOM SAMPLE

The population is segmented into more than one layer ("stratum") and items are randomly selected within each layer. Here, every item in the population has a chance (not necessarily equal) of being included in the sample. This approach is normally used to reduce the overall sample size in populations with large variances. It is also commonly used in risk abatement strategies, where more weight is given toward selecting samples from the strata containing the highest risk.

SYSTEMATIC SAMPLING

Samples are selected based upon a pre-defined sequence and are selected as they're being produced by the process. Systematic sampling is usually used to select samples from manufacturing processes for process monitoring and control and in transactional settings, such as customer transactions in a bank.

Formulas Used for Determining Sample Size

Formula for estimating sample size when using attributes data:

$$n = \left(\frac{2Z_{(\alpha/2)}}{\omega}\right)^2 \cdot p \cdot q$$

where:

n is the sample size

Z is the z-value associated with the desired confidence level

ω is the desired precision of the estimate

p is the population proportion (use 0.5 if unknown)

q is equal to $(1 - p)$

Example: How large of a sample is required to estimate the proportion of incorrect invoices with a sample precision of +/– 2% at the 95% confidence level?

$$n = \left(\frac{2 \cdot 1.96}{0.04}\right)^2 \cdot 0.5 \cdot 0.5 = 2,401$$

In order for your sample estimate to be within +/– 2% of the actual population value with 95% confidence, 2,401 items must be selected randomly from the population of interest.

Formula for estimating sample size when using variables data:

$$n = \left(\frac{2Z_{(\alpha/2)}\sigma}{\omega}\right)^2$$

where:

n is the sample size

Z is the z-value associated with the desired confidence level (see Table 3-2) ω is the desired precision of the sample

σ is the population standard deviation (or estimate of σ)

COMMONLY USED CONFIDENCE LEVELS

Confidence Level	$Z_{(\alpha/2)}$ Value
99%	2.58
95%	1.96
90%	1.65
80%	1.28

Table 3-2.

Example: How large of a sample is required to estimate the average value of outstanding invoices within +/- $10 at the 90% confidence level, given a standard deviation of $65?

$$n = \left(\frac{2 \cdot 1.65 \cdot \$65}{\$20} \right)^2 = 115$$

In order for your sample estimate to be within +/- $10 of the actual population average with 90% confidence, 115 items must be selected randomly from the population of interest.

Allocating Samples for Stratified Random Sampling

After determining your sample size, you may desire to select portions of your sample from different groups (strata) within the population. Reasons for stratification are:

1. *Risk Reduction*: e.g., when sampling finished goods inventory, a larger proportion of high value items are sampled to reduce financial risk.
2. *Reduction of Sample Size*: homogeneous populations (low variance) require smaller sample sizes than do heterogeneous populations (high variance). Stratification of heterogeneous populations into smaller, more homogeneous groups for sampling will reduce the overall sample size required for a given level of estimating precision.

Two approaches for stratifying a population are presented below. The first is a risk-based allocation approach that may be used with both attributes and variables data. The second, used with variables data (Neyman Allocation Method), weights the sample using stratum variance (higher variance strata are weighted more than lower variance strata).

RISK-BASED ALLOCATION APPROACH

This approach requires a strategy for allocating samples to strata based on reducing risk. A risk scale from 1 to 10 (1 is lowest, 10 is highest risk) is used and the allocation proportions are calculated by dividing the risk rating by the sum of the risk ratings. In the example below, Account A is allocated 0.15 of the total (3 ÷ 20).

Example: The risk based allocation approach for a sample of 115 transactions is shown in Table 3.3. The allocation proportions were calculated as follows: 17 samples will be taken from A (0.15 X 115), 40 will be taken from B (0.35 X 115), 6 will be taken from C (0.05 X 115), and 52 will be taken from D (0.45 X 115).

RISK-BASED SAMPLE ALLOCATION

Account Type	Risk Rating	Allocation Proportion	Sample Size
A	3	0.15	17
B	7	0.35	40
C	1	0.05	6
D	9	0.45	52
Total	20	1.00	115

Table 3-3.

NEYMAN ALLOCATION METHOD

This method is used for sample allocation based on stratum variance and helps ensure adequate coverage across all strata.

Formula for estimating sample size using the Neyman allocation method:

$$n_i = n \left(\frac{N_i \sigma_i}{\sum_{i=1}^{k} N_i \sigma_i} \right)$$

where:

N_i is the stratum size

σ_i is the standard deviation stratum for stratum i

n_i is the sample allocation size for stratum i

n is the total sample size

Example: A sample allocation using the Neyman approach for a random sample of 230 observations is shown in Table 3.4.

NEYMAN SAMPLE ALLOCATION

N_i	σ_i	$N_i\sigma_i$	$N_i\sigma_i/\Sigma N_i\sigma_i$	n_i
1550	5	7750	0.37	85
620	15	9300	0.44	102
393	10	3930	0.19	43
	Sums	20980	1.00	230

Table 3-4.

Determining Sample Sizes for Hypothesis Tests

When using sampling for hypothesis testing, we usually consider two types of risks associated with making a bad decision: *alpha risk* (α) and *beta risk* (β). *Alpha risk* is the probability of rejecting the null hypothesis when it is true and beta risk is the probability of accepting the null hypothesis when it is false. In practice, we define our tolerance for both α and β risk and factor it into our sample size equation.

Formula for estimating sample size for hypothesis testing:

$$n = \left((Z_{(\alpha/2)} + Z_{(\beta)}) \frac{\sigma}{\delta} \right)^2$$

where:

is the sample size

is the z-value associated with the desired alpha risk (use $_{\alpha/2)}$ for t-tests)

$_{(\beta)}$ is the z-value associated with the desired beta risk (use $_{\beta)}$ for t-tests)

is the standard deviation

is the difference that we wish to detect

Example: What sample size is required to detect a difference of 5 or more in the process average? The standard deviation is 10 and the desired alpha risk is 0.05 and beta risk is 0.10.

$$n = \left((1.96 + 1.28)\, \frac{10}{5} \right)^2 = 42$$

In order to detect a difference in the process average of 5 or more with an alpha risk of 0.05 and a beta risk of 0.10, a random sample of 42 observations is required.

How to Estimate Sample Size

1. Define the purpose for the sampling.
2. Specify the type of data that will be collected, i.e., discrete or continuous.
3. Select the appropriate sampling technique: simple random sampling, systematic sampling, or stratified sampling.
4. If stratification is desired, select the appropriate allocation method: Risk based or Neyman allocation method.
5. Specify the desired precision interval and confidence level.

6. Specify the population parameters: proportion for discrete data and standard deviation for continuous data.
7. Use appropriate sample size formula: select attributes, variables, or hypothesis test formula.

CHAPTER FOUR
Confidence Intervals

What Is a Confidence Interval?

When we use statistics to estimate the value of a population parameter (e.g., mean), we calculate what's known as a *point estimate*. The probability that a point estimate will exactly equal the population value is infinitely small. To account for this drawback, we calculate a *confidence interval*, which assigns a probability that the actual population value is contained within a specified range of values.

For example, if we calculated a 95% confidence interval of the mean as being in the range of 20 to 35, we can interpret this as a 0.95 probability that the actual population mean is somewhere between 20 and 35.

Application of Confidence Intervals in Six Sigma

In *Six Sigma*, confidence intervals are used to determine baseline performance levels, compare process performance with multiple factors (e.g., different machines, people, time periods), estimate defect levels, etc.

Confidence Interval for the Mean

When we're interested in determining an interval estimate of the mean of a population, we need to select the appropriate formula. If we know the standard deviation of the population we use the formula for *mean estimation—σ known*. When the standard deviation is not known, use the formula for *mean estimation—σ unknown*.

MEAN ESTIMATION—STANDARD DEVIATION (σ) IS KNOWN

To estimate confidence intervals for the population mean, we use the following formula:

$$\overline{x} - \frac{Z_{(\alpha/2)}\sigma}{\sqrt{n}} \leq \mu \leq \overline{x} + \frac{Z_{(\alpha/2)}\sigma}{\sqrt{n}}$$

where:

μ is the population mean

$\overline{x}$ is the estimate of the population mean

Z is the value associated with the desired confidence level

σ is the population standard deviation

n is the sample size

Example: You're interested in estimating the average miles per gallon (mpg) for a newly purchased car. With a sample of n = 30, you calculate an average of 27.5 mpg. Using Excel calculate the 95% confidence interval estimate for your new car, given that σ = 2.5 mpg?

CONFIDENCE(0.05, 2.5, 30)

Returns the value, 0.89, which is equivalent to:

$$\frac{Z_{(\alpha/2)}\sigma}{\sqrt{n}} = \pm 0.89$$

Therefore, $\mu = \overline{x} \pm 0.89$ and the 95% confidence interval estimate is:

$$26.6 \text{ mpg} \leq \mu \leq 28.4 \text{ mpg}$$

You can expect your new car to average 26.6 mpg to 28.4 mpg.

MEAN ESTIMATION—STANDARD DEVIATION (σ) UNKNOWN

If the population σ is unknown, we estimate it and substitute s with s in the formula:

$$\bar{x} - \frac{t_{(\alpha/2)}s}{\sqrt{n}} \leq \mu \leq \bar{x} + \frac{t_{(\alpha/2)}s}{\sqrt{n}}$$

Example: You're interested in estimating the average drying time in minutes for a new "quick drying" paint. You use five paint samples to estimate average drying time and standard deviation. The results are: average drying time = 180 minutes and standard deviation = 10 minutes. What is the 90% confidence interval estimate for average paint drying time?

Excel doesn't have a function for this situation. Here's how to get around that limitation. Use (1 – confidence) and (n–1) in the Excel formula below to determine the $t_{(\alpha/2)}$ value.

$$\text{TINV}(0.1, 4) = 2.13$$

which is then used in the formula:

$$\frac{t_{(\alpha/2)}s}{\sqrt{n}} = \frac{(2.13)(10)}{\sqrt{5}} = \pm 9.53$$

Therefore, $\mu = \bar{x} \pm 9.53$ and the 90% confidence interval estimate is:

$$170.5 \text{ minutes} \leq \mu \leq 189.5 \text{ minutes}$$

The average drying time of the new paint is between 170.5 minutes and 189.5 minutes.

Confidence Interval for Proportions

To estimate confidence intervals for population proportions, we use the following formula:

$$\hat{p} - Z_{(\alpha/2)} \sqrt{\frac{\hat{p}(1-\hat{p})}{n}} \leq p \leq \hat{p} + Z_{(\alpha/2)} \sqrt{\frac{\hat{p}(1-\hat{p})}{n}}$$

where:

p is the population proportion
$\hat{p}$ is the estimate of the population proportion
Z is the value associated with the desired confidence level
n is the sample size

Example: Using Excel, estimate the 95% confidence interval estimate for the proportion of incomplete credit card applications, given that 33 incomplete applications were found in a random sample of 200?

The sample estimate of the proportion of incomplete applications is calculated as:

$$\hat{p} = \frac{33}{200} = 0.165$$

$$NORMSINV(0.975)$$

Returns the value 1.96, which is used in the formula:

$$\hat{p} \pm Z_{(\alpha/2)} \sqrt{\frac{\hat{p}(1-\hat{p})}{n}} = 0.165 \pm 1.96 \sqrt{\frac{0.165(1-0.165)}{200}}$$

Therefore, p = 0.165 ± 0.051 and the 95% confidence interval is: $0.114 \leq p \leq 0.216$

The proportion of incomplete applications is a value between 0.114 and 0.216.

Confidence Interval for the Variance of a Normal Distribution

To estimate confidence intervals for the population variance, we use the following formula:

$$\frac{(n-1)s^2}{\chi^2_{(\alpha/2),\, n-1}} \leq \sigma^2 \leq \frac{(n-1)s^2}{\chi^2_{(1-\alpha/2),\, n-1}}$$

where:

σ^2 is the population variance

s^2 is the estimate of the population variance

χ^2 is the chi-square value associated with the desired confidence level

n is the sample size

Example: You're interested in estimating the population variance for the assembly of custom circuit boards. The sample variance is 10 minutes^2 and the sample size is n = 100. Using Excel, calculate the 95% confidence interval estimate for in circuit board assembly variance.

Using Excel, determine $\chi^2_{(\alpha/2)}$ and $\chi^2_{(1-\alpha/2)}$:

$$\text{CHIINV}(0.025,99)$$
$$\chi^2_{(\alpha/2)} = 128.4$$

$$\text{CHIINV}(0.975,99)$$
$$\chi^2_{(1-\alpha/2)} = 73.4$$

Substitute the χ^2 values in the formula:

$$\frac{(100-1)10}{128.4} \leq \sigma^2 \leq \frac{(100-1)10}{73.4}$$

The 95% confidence interval estimate is:
$$7.7 \leq \sigma^2 \leq 13.5$$

The population variance for circuit board assembly is between 7.7 and 13.5. Therefore, the assembly operation's standard deviation is between 2.8 minutes and 3.7 minutes.

How to Determine Confidence Intervals

1. Determine sample size.
2. Select random sample.
3. Specify confidence level $(1-\alpha)$.
4. Select the appropriate formula (mean, proportion, or variance).
5. Calculate confidence interval and interpret results.

CHAPTER FIVE
Hypothesis Testing

What Is Hypothesis Testing?

Hypothesis testing is the application of statistics to confirm or disallow a theory about the value of some population parameter. Hypothesis tests can be used to make decisions about any process that we can sample. Examples of hypothesis testing applications are: average customer waiting time in a bank, variance of percent lead in a gasoline formulation, average diameter of ball bearings, etc.

Application of Hypothesis Testing in Six Sigma

In *Six Sigma*, hypothesis tests are used to evaluate actual process performance (average and variation) relative to a standard or specification, to determine if differences exist between processes, to verify process improvement by comparing before and after data, etc.

Types of Hypothesis Tests

Hypothesis tests employ two opposed conditions: the null hypothesis (H_o) and the alternate hypothesis (H_a). The null hypothesis asserts that there is no difference between the sample value and the population parameter being tested. The alternate hypothesis asserts that there is a difference between the sample value and the population parameter being tested. Hypothesis tests are either one-tailed or two-tailed.

TWO-TAILED HYPOTHESIS TESTS

Two-tailed tests are used to determine if a parameter, such as process average or variance, is equal to a specified value. These tests are stated in terms of a null hypothesis (H_0) and an alternate hypothesis (H_a) as shown below.

$$H_0: \Phi = x$$
$$H_a: \Phi \neq x$$

where:

Φ is the parameter being tested

x is some specified value

Example: The hypothesis test for average waiting time in an amusement park being equal to 15 minutes is stated as:

$$H_0: \mu = 15 \text{ minutes}$$
$$H_a: \mu \neq 15 \text{ minutes}$$

ONE-TAILED HYPOTHESIS TESTS

With one-tailed tests, one-of-two possible alternate hypotheses must be selected. The alternate hypothesis is stated as an inequality; either as "less-than" or "greater than."

$$H_0: \Phi = x$$
$$H_a: \Phi < x \quad \text{or} \quad H_a: \Phi > x$$

where:

Φ is the parameter being tested

x is some specified value

Example 1: The hypothesis test for average waiting time in an amusement park being less than 15 minutes is stated as:

$$H_0: \mu = 15 \text{ minutes}$$
$$H_a: \mu < 15 \text{ minutes}$$

Example 2: The hypothesis test for average waiting time being greater than 15 minutes is stated as:

$$H_o: \mu = 15 \text{ minutes}$$
$$H_a: \mu > 15 \text{ minutes}$$

Decision Errors and Hypothesis Testing

Since the decision to accept or reject H_o is based on a sample estimate, it is possible to arrive at an incorrect decision. The two types of errors that can occur when performing a hypothesis test are referred to as *Type I* and *Type II* errors.

TYPE I ERROR

This type of error occurs when we reject H_o when it is true. The probability of committing a *Type I* error is called alpha (α) risk.

Example: From sample data, we conclude that a call center's average response time is greater than its performance target, when it is actually lower than the target.

TYPE II ERROR

This type of error occurs when we accept H_o when it is not true. The probability of committing a *Type II* error is called beta (ß) risk.

Example: We conclude from sample data that a call center's average response time is meeting target, when it is actually exceeding the target.

Significance Level and the Power of the Hypothesis Test

The *significance level* of a hypothesis test is the probability that we assign for the occurrence of a *Type I* error, i.e., *alpha risk* (α). Power is the probability of correctly rejecting H_o when it is false and is defined as $(1 - \beta)$. We control *alpha risk* directly because we specify the *significance level* of the test. We cannot directly control the *power* of the test because *beta risk* is influenced by sample size. The larger our sample size becomes, the smaller is our *beta risk*, with a corresponding increase in the power of the test. Figure 5-1 illustrates the relationship of alpha risk, beta risk, and power

RELATIONSHIP BETWEEN α, β, AND POWER

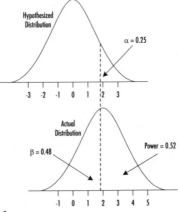

Figure 5-1

Decision Rules

The decision to accept or reject H_0 depends upon the value of our parameter estimate relative to the z-value that corresponds to the significance level that we have chosen (refer to Table 5-1). The significance level is equal to α for *one-tail tests* or $\alpha/2$ for *two-tail tests*.

Figure 5-2 shows a two-tail hypothesis test, with z-values (-z and z) defined by $\alpha/2$ (this is our hypothetical distribution). If our sample estimate is within the bounds of -z and z, we can accept H_0 as being true.

Figure 5-3 shows a one-tail hypothesis test with a "greater-than" alternative hypothesis and Figure 5-4 shows a one-tail "less-than" alternative hypothesis.

TWO-TAIL HYPOTHESIS TEST

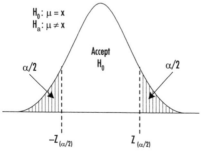

Figure 5-2.

One-Tail Hypothesis Test, Greater-Than Alternative

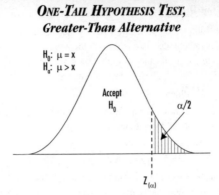

H_0: $\mu = x$
H_a: $\mu > x$

Accept H_0

$\alpha/2$

$Z_{(\alpha)}$

Figure 5-3.

One-Tail Hypothesis Test, Less-Than Alternative

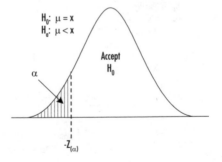

H_0: $\mu = x$
H_a: $\mu < x$

Accept H_0

α

$-Z_{(\alpha)}$

Figure 5-4.

The decision rules for hypothesis tests are:

1. If the $|Z < Z_{(\alpha)}|$, accept H_o

2. If the $|Z > Z_{(\alpha)}|$, reject H_o

CONVERTING ALPHA RISK TO Z-VALUES

Table 5-1 shows the most commonly used alpha risk values with their corresponding z-values and confidence levels.

ALPHA RISK AND Z-VALUES

Alpha Risk	Two-Tail Z-value $(\alpha/2)$	One-Tail Z-value (α)	Confidence Level
0.100	1.64	1.28	90.0%
0.050	1.96	1.64	95.0%
0.025	2.24	1.96	97.5%
0.010	2.58	2.33	99.0%

Table 5-1.

P-VALUES

Most statistical software packages report p-values with hypothesis test output.

Figure 5-5 illustrates the relationship between a sample estimate ($\bar{x}$) and its corresponding p-value, for a hypothesis test of the mean.

P-VALUE AND α

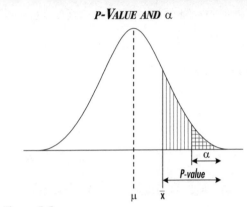

Figure 5-5.

The p-value is the smallest value of α for which we would have rejected H₀. In this case, it is the area under the curve that is to the right of the sample value.

When using p-values, the decision rules are:

1. If the p-value is greater than α, *do not reject* H₀.
2. If the p-value is less than α, *reject* H₀.

Example: A sample was used to estimate the average flow rate through a water filter that is rated for 13.0 gallons-per-minute. The sample's average flow rate is 12.5 gallons-per-minute, with a p-value of 0.04.

Do you accept or reject the null hypothesis (H₀: no difference between sample average and filter rating vs. Hₐ: difference between sample average and filter rating), with α = 0.10?

Since the p-value (0.04) is less than $\alpha/2=0.05$, we must reject H_0 (note that if our original α value were 0.01, we would not reject H_0 with an α value of 0.04.

Hypothesis Tests of the Mean

z-Test

The z-test is used to compare a sample average to a specified value when the standard deviation is known.

The formula for the z-test is:

$$z = \frac{\overline{x} - \mu}{\dfrac{\sigma}{\sqrt{n}}}$$

where:

z is the test statistic
$\overline{x}$ is the sample average
μ is the specified value
σ is the known standard deviation
n is the sample size

Example 1: The target average diameter for an electrical conduit is 10.2 cm, with a known $s = 0.5$ cm. The average diameter from a sample of $n = 25$ is 10.0 cm. Is the process average on-target (use $\alpha = 0.05$)?

This is a two-tail test. State the hypotheses (H_0 and H_a), *calculate z, and compare to* $Z_{(\alpha/2)}$.

$H_0 : \mu = 10.0$ cm

$H_a : \mu \neq 10.0$ cm

$Z_{(\alpha/2)} = 1.96$ (from Table 5-1)

Solve for Z:

$$Z = \frac{10.2 - 10.0}{\frac{0.5}{\sqrt{25}}} = 2$$

Since $|Z > Z_{(\alpha/2)}|$, we reject H_0, the process is not on-target.

Example 2: Evaluate the process in Example 1 using the p-value method.

A look at Table 5-2 shows that $p=0.040$. Since $p < \alpha$, we reject H_0.

Z-TEST OUTPUT

Test of $\mu = 10$ vs μ not = 10 The assumed $\sigma = 0.5$			
Variable	**N**	**Mean**	**St Dev**	**SE Mean**
Diameter	25	10.206	0.564	0.100
Variable	**95.0% CI**		**Z**	**P**
Diameter	10.010	10.402	2.06	0.040

Table 5-2.

TWO-SAMPLE Z-TEST

The two-sample z-test is used to compare the means of two processes when their standard deviations are known. Use the two-sample z-test when comparing two independent populations.

The formula for the two-sample z-test is:

$$Z_{ts} = \frac{(\bar{x}_1 - \bar{x}_2)}{\sqrt{\dfrac{\sigma_1^2}{n_1} + \dfrac{\sigma_2^2}{n_2}}}$$

where:

Z_{ts} is the test statistic

$\bar{x}_1$ is the sample average for process 1

$\bar{x}_2$ is the sample average for process 2

σ_1^2 is the variance for process 1

σ_2^2 is the variance for process 2

n_1 is the sample size for process 1

n_2 is the sample size for process 2

Example: Two stamping machines have a known standard deviation of 2.0 pounds per inch^2 pressure. Determine if these two machines operate at the same average pounds per inch^2 pressure, using $\alpha = 0.05$. A sample of 10 stampings from each machine resulted in an average pound per inch^2 pressure of 51.2 for machine 1 and 50.9 for machine 2.

This is a two-tail test. State the hypotheses (H_0 and H_a), calculate z_{ts}, and compare to $Z_{(\alpha/2)}$.

$H_0: \mu_1 - \mu_2 = 0$ (same average)

$H_a: \mu_1 - \mu_2 \neq 0$ (different average)

$Z_{(\alpha/2)} = 1.96$ (from Table 5-1)

Solve for Z_{ts}:

$$Z_{ts} = \frac{(51.2 - 50.9)}{\sqrt{\dfrac{4}{10} + \dfrac{4}{10}}} = 0.34$$

Since $|Z_{ts} < Z_{(\alpha/2)}|$, we accept H_0, the two processes are operating at the same average pounds per inch^2 of pressure.

PAIRED Z-TEST

The paired z-test is used to compare the average difference between two samples when their standard deviations are known. Use the paired z-test when comparing two alternatives that are not independent (e.g., you suspect that a systematic factor that is either unknown or can't be controlled that may be affecting the process average).

The formula for the paired z-test is:

$$Z_p = \frac{\overline{d} - \delta}{\sigma_{\overline{d}}}$$

where:

Z_p is the test statistic
$\overline{d}$ is the average difference between sample pairs
δ is the hypothesized paired difference
$\sigma_{\overline{d}}$ is the standard error of paired differences

Example: Six finance clerks were used to test the performance of two different accounts payable systems. The metric used to assess performance was the average number of transactions per day. The data was paired to account for the differences in the clerks (see Table 5-3). Is there a difference in he systems (use $\alpha = 0.10$)?

This is a two-tail test. State the hypotheses (H_0 and H_a), calculate Z_{ts}, and compare to $Z_{(\alpha/2)}$.

H_0: $\delta = 0$ (no difference exists)

H_a: $\delta \neq 0$ (difference exists)

$Z_{(\alpha/2)} = 1.64$ (from Table 5-1)

PAIRED Z-TEST RESULTS

Clerk	System 1 (Trans/Day)	System 2 (Trans/Day)	Difference
A	200	250	50
B	190	260	70
C	220	230	10
D	150	170	20
E	210	210	0
F	180	230	50
		$\overline{d} =$	33.3
		$\sigma_d =$	27.3

Table 5-3.

Calculate $\sigma_{\bar{d}}$ and solve for Z_p:

$$\sigma_{\bar{d}} = \frac{\sigma_d}{\sqrt{n}} = \frac{27.3}{\sqrt{6}} = 11.2$$

$$Z_p = \frac{27.3 - 0}{11.2} = 2.4$$

Since $|Z_p > Z_{(\alpha/2)}|$, we reject H_0. System 2 produces a greater number of transactions per day than System 1.

t-Test

The t-test is used to compare a sample to a specified value when the standard deviation is unknown.

The formula for the t-test is:

$$t = \frac{\bar{x} - \mu}{\frac{s}{\sqrt{n}}}$$

where:

t is the test statistic
$\bar{x}$ is the sample average
μ is the standard value
s is the sample standard deviation
n is the sample size

The t-test employs the t-distribution, which is derived from the normal distribution. Its shape depends on sample size (n). The t-distribution is equivalent to the normal distribution when $n = \infty$. Use Table 5-4 for t-tests (note that Table 5-4 employs sample size (n) rather than the traditional degrees of freedom).

Example 1: A carbonated beverage filling operation has a long-term average fill volume of 16.2 ounces. An average of 16.1 ounces and s = 0.1 ounces was calculated from a sample (n = 15 bottles). Using α = 0.10, determine if the average fill volume is less than the historical average.

This is a one-tail test. State the hypotheses (H_0 and H_a), calculate t, and compare to $t_{(\alpha)}$.

H_0: μ = 16.2 ounces

H_a: μ < 16.2 ounces

$t_{(\alpha)}$ = 1.345 (from Table 5-4)

Solve for t:

$$ t = \frac{16.12 - 16.20}{\frac{0.09}{\sqrt{15}}} = -3.4 $$

Since $|t > t_{(\alpha)}|$, we reject H_0, the process average has shifted and the bottle volume is less than the historical average.

COMMON VALUES OF THE t-DISTRIBUTION

	One-Tail			Two-Tail		
	α			α/2		
n	0.10	0.05	0.025	0.10	0.05	0.025
2	3.078	6.314	12.706	6.314	12.706	25.452
3	1.886	2.920	4.303	2.920	4.303	6.205
4	1.638	2.353	3.182	2.353	3.182	4.177
5	1.533	2.132	2.776	2.132	2.776	3.495
6	1.476	2.015	2.571	2.015	2.571	3.163
7	1.440	1.943	2.447	1.943	2.447	2.969
8	1.415	1.895	2.365	1.895	2.365	2.841
9	1.397	1.860	2.306	1.860	2.306	2.752
10	1.383	1.833	2.262	1.833	2.262	2.685
11	1.372	1.812	2.228	1.812	2.228	2.634
12	1.363	1.796	2.201	1.796	2.201	2.593
13	1.356	1.782	2.179	1.782	2.179	2.560
14	1.350	1.771	2.160	1.771	2.160	2.533
15	1.345	1.761	2.145	1.761	2.145	2.510
16	1.341	1.753	2.131	1.753	2.131	2.490
17	1.337	1.746	2.120	1.746	2.120	2.473
18	1.333	1.740	2.110	1.740	2.110	2.458
19	1.330	1.734	2.101	1.734	2.101	2.445
20	1.328	1.729	2.093	1.729	2.093	2.433

Table 5-4. (Continued on next page)

COMMON VALUES OF THE T-DISTRIBUTION

	One-Tail			Two-Tail		
	α			α/2		
n	0.10	0.05	0.025	0.10	0.05	0.025
21	1.325	1.725	2.086	1.725	2.086	2.423
22	1.323	1.721	2.080	1.721	2.080	2.414
23	1.321	1.717	2.074	1.717	2.074	2.405
24	1.319	1.714	2.069	1.714	2.069	2.398
25	1.318	1.711	2.064	1.711	2.064	2.391
26	1.316	1.708	2.060	1.708	2.060	2.385
27	1.315	1.706	2.056	1.706	2.056	2.379
28	1.314	1.703	2.052	1.703	2.052	2.373
29	1.313	1.701	2.048	1.701	2.048	2.368
30	1.311	1.699	2.045	1.699	2.045	2.364
40	1.304	1.685	2.023	1.685	2.023	2.331
50	1.299	1.667	2.010	1.667	2.010	2.312
60	1.296	1.671	2.001	1.671	2.001	2.300
70	1.294	1.667	1.995	1.667	1.995	2.291
80	1.292	1.664	1.990	1.664	1.990	2.285
90	1.291	1.662	1.987	1.662	1.987	2.280
100	1.290	1.660	1.984	1.660	1.984	2.276
∞	1.282	1.645	1.960	1.645	1.960	2.242

Table 5-4. (Continued)

Example 2: Evaluate the process in Example 1 using the p-value method.

Table 5-5 shows that p = 0.002. Since p < α, we reject H$_0$.

T-TEST OUTPUT

Test of μ = 16.2 vs μ < 16.2			
Variable	**N**	**Mean**	**St Dev**	**SE Mean**
Vol	15	16.1220	0.889	0.0229
Variable	**95.0% Upper Bound**		**T**	**P**
Vol		16.1625		--3.40	0.002

Table 5-5.

TWO-SAMPLE T-TEST

The two-sample t-test is used to compare the means of two processes when the standard deviations are unknown. Use the two-sample t-test when sampling from two independent populations.

The formula for the two-sample t-test is:

$$t_{ts} = \frac{(\bar{x}_1 - \bar{x}_2)}{S_p \sqrt{\frac{1}{n_1} + \frac{1}{n_2}}}$$

where:

t_{ts} is the test statistic
$\bar{x}_1$ is the sample average for process 1
$\bar{x}_2$ is the sample average for process 2

S_p is the pooled standard deviation

n_1 is the sample size for process 1

n_2 is the sample size for process 2

The formula for pooled standard deviation is:

$$S_p = \sqrt{\frac{s_1^2(n_1-1) + s_2^2(n_2-1)}{(n_1-1) + (n_2-1)}}$$

where:

s_1^2 is the variance for process 1

s_2^2 is the variance for process 2

Example 1: Two automated filling machine are used to package cooking oil in 32 ounce plastic bottles. Samples are selected from both fillers, giving the following results:

FILLER SAMPLING RESULTS

Filler	N	Averages (Ounces)	Standard Deviation
1	9	32.4	0.99
2	16	31.9	1.04

Table 5-6.

Using $\alpha = 0.05$, determine if the average fill volume is the same for both fillers.

This is a two-tail test. State the hypotheses (H_0 and H_a), calculate t_{ts}, and compare to $t_{(\alpha/2)}$. When using Table 5-4 for two-sample t-test, $n = n_1 + n_2$.

H_0: $\mu_1 - \mu_2 = 0$ (same average)

H_a: $\mu_1 - \mu_2 \neq 0$ (different average)

$t_{(\alpha/2)} = 2.06$ (from Table 5-4)

Determine the pooled standard deviation and solve for t_{ts}:

$$s_p = \frac{(0.98)(8) + (1.08)(15)}{(8 + 15)} = 1.02$$

$$t_{ts} = \frac{(32.4 - 31.9)}{1.02 \sqrt{\frac{1}{9} + \frac{1}{16}}} = 1.18$$

Since $|t_{ts} < t_{(\alpha/2)}|$, we accept H_0, the two processes have the same average fill level.

Example 2: Evaluate the process in Example 1 using the p-value method.

Table 5-7 shows that $p = 0.239$. Since $p > \alpha$, we cannot reject H_0.

TWO-SAMPLE T-TEST OUTPUT

Two-Sample of T for Filler_1 v Filler_2				
	N	Mean	St Dev	SE Mean
Filler_1	9	32.393	0.991	0.33
Filler_2	16	31.88	1.04	0.26
Difference = mu Filler_1 – mu Filler_2				
Estimate for difference: 0.517				
95% CI for difference: (–0.367, 1.400)				
T-Test of difference = 0 (vs. not =): T-Value = 1.21				
P-Value = 0.239 DF = 23				
Both use Pooled StDev = 1.03				

Table 5-7.

PAIRED T-TEST

The paired t-test is used to compare the average difference between two samples when their standard deviations are unknown. Use the paired t-test when comparing two alternatives that are not independent.

The formula for the paired t-test is:

$$t_p = \frac{\bar{d} - \delta}{S_{\bar{d}}}$$

where:

t_p is the test statistic
$\bar{d}$ is the average difference between sample pairs
δ is the hypothesized paired difference
$S_{\bar{d}}$ is the standard error of the paired differences

Example 1: We are interested in comparing the yield performance of two machines that are used to extrude steel wire. Since the tensile strength of the wire used in the process varies greatly, a paired t-test is selected to perform the comparison. Table 5-8 shows the test data. Use $\alpha = 0.05$.

PAIRED T-TEST DATA

Extruder_1	Extruder_2	Differences
92.3	93.2	0.9
90.5	83.7	−6.8
91.9	90.8	−1.1
91.7	91.8	0.1
94.9	88.7	−6.2
93.6	90.7	−2.9
90.5	93.8	3.3
93.3	91.0	−2.3
94.4	91.3	−3.1
	$\bar{d} =$	−2.0
	$S\bar{d} =$	3.3

Table 5-8.

This is a two-tail test. State the hypotheses (H_0 and H_a), calculate t_p, and compare to $t_{(\alpha/2)}$.

H_0: $\delta = 0$ (no difference exists)

H_a: $\delta \neq 0$ (difference exists)

$t_{(\alpha/2)} = 2.11$ (from Table 5-4)

Calculate $S_{\bar{d}}$ and solve for t_p:

$$S_{\bar{d}} = \frac{S_d}{\sqrt{n}} = \frac{3.3}{\sqrt{9}} = 1.1$$

$$t_p = \frac{-2.0 - 0}{1.1} = -1.86$$

Since $|t_p < t_{(\alpha/2)}|$, we accept H_0. There is no evidence of a difference in average yield between the two extruders.

Example 2: Evaluate the process in Example 1 using the p-value method.

Table 5-9 shows that $p = 0.100$. Since $p > \alpha$, we cannot reject H_0.

PAIRED T-TEST OUTPUT

Paired T for Extruder_1 − Extruder_2				
	N	Mean	St Dev	SE Mean
Extruder_1	9	92.567	1.590	0.530
Extruder_2	9	90.556	2.965	0.988
Difference	9	2.01	3.25	1.08
95% CI for mean difference: (−0.49, 4.51)				
T-Test of mean difference = 0 (v. not = 0): T-Value = 1.86				
P-Value = 0.100				

Table 5-9.

Hypothesis Tests of Proportions

SINGLE PROPORTION TEST

The single proportion test is used to compare a binomial proportion to a specified value.

The formula for the proportions test is:

$$\text{When } x < np_0 \Rightarrow Z_0 = \frac{(X + 0.05) - np_0}{\sqrt{np_0(1 - p_0)}}$$

$$\text{When } x > np_0 \Rightarrow Z_0 = \frac{(X - 0.05) - np_0}{\sqrt{np_0(1 - p_0)}}$$

where:

Z_0 is the test statistic
x is the random variable
p_0 is the specified value
n is the sample size

xample 1: A sample of pistons (n = 50) was tested to etermine the proportion of nonconforming product con-ined 4 defects. Historically, the proportion of nonconform-g product has been 0.05. Has the proportion nonconform-g product decreased? Use $\alpha = 0.025$.

This is a one-tail test. State the hypotheses (H_0 and H_a), lculate Z_0, and compare to $Z_{(\alpha)}$.

H_0: p = 0.05

H_a: p < 0.05

$Z_{(\alpha)} = 1.96$ (from Table 5-1)

Solve for Z_0:

$$Z_0 = \frac{(4 + 0.05) - (300)(0.05)}{\sqrt{(300)(0.05)(1 - 0.05)}} = -2.9$$

Since $|Z_0 > Z_{(\alpha)}|$, we reject H_0. The proportion noncon-rming product has decreased.

xample 2: Evaluate the process in Example 1 using the p-lue method.

Table 5-10 shows that p = 0.002. Since p < α, we reject .

SINGLE PROPORTION OUTPUT

X	N	Sample p	95.0%	Upper Bound	Z-Value	P-Value
4	300	0.013333		0.024226	−2.91	0.002

able 5-10.

TWO-SAMPLE PROPORTION TEST

The two-sample proportion test is used to perform a binomial comparison of two samples.

The formula for the two-sample proportion test is:

$$Z_0 = \frac{p_1 - p_2}{\sqrt{\hat{p}(1-\hat{p})\left(\dfrac{1}{n_1} + \dfrac{1}{n_2}\right)}}$$

given:

$$\hat{p} = \frac{n_1 p_1 + n_2 p_2}{n_1 + n_2}$$

where:

Z_0 is the test statistic
$\hat{p}$ is the estimated proportion
p_1 is sample proportion 1
p_2 is sample proportion 2
n_1 is the sample size for p_1
n_2 is the sample size for p_2

Example 1: A sample of 150 invoices that was taken prior implementation of process improvements, showed a 9% occurrence of incorrect invoices. Three months after the implementation of those improvements, a sample of 250 invoices resulted in a 6% error rate. Has the error rate been reduced (use $\alpha = 0.05$)?

This is a one-tail test. State the hypotheses (H_0 and H_α), calculate Z_0, and compare to $Z_{(\alpha)}$.

$H_0: p_2 = p_1$
$H_a: p_2 < p_1$

$Z_{(\alpha)} = 1.65$ (from Table 5-1)

Calculate $\hat{p}$ and solve for Z_0:

$$\hat{p} = \frac{(150)(0.087) + (250)(0.060)}{150 + 250} = 0.70$$

$$Z_0 = \frac{0.086 - 0.060}{\sqrt{(0.07)(0.93)(1/150 + 1/250)}} = 0.97$$

Since $|Z_0 < Z_{(\alpha)}|$, we cannot reject H_0. There is not enough evidence of a difference in the proportion of incorrect invoices after the process improvements were implemented.

Example 2: Evaluate the process in Example 1 using the p-value method.

Table 5-11 shows that $p = 0.331$. Since $p > \alpha$, we cannot reject H_0.

Two-Sample Proportion Output

Test of T for Filler_1 v Filler_2			
Variable	X	N	Sample P
Before	13	150	0.086667
After	15	250	0.060000
Estimate for p(Before) -- p(After): 0.0266667 95% CI for p(Before) -- p(After): (--0.0271272, 0.0804606) Test for p(Before) -- p(After) = 0 (vs not = 0): Z = 0.97 p-Value = 0.331			

Table 5-11.

Hypothesis Tests of Variance

χ^2 TEST

The χ^2 test is used to compare a sample variance to a specified value.

The formula for the χ^2 test is:

$$\chi^2 = (n-1)\frac{s^2}{\sigma_0^2}$$

where:
χ^2 is the test statistic
n is the sample size
s is the sample standard deviation
σ_0^2 is the specified value

Example: The standard deviation for the temperature of a stable plastic injection molding process is 5.5°F. After an adjustment was made to the process, the standard deviation of a sample of ten measurements is 6.3°F. Has the standard deviation of the process increased (use $\alpha = 0.025$)?

This is a one-tail test. State the hypotheses (H_0 and H_a), calculate χ^2, and compare to $\chi^2_{(\alpha)}$.

H_0: $\sigma_2 = \sigma_0^2$

H_a: $\sigma^2 < \sigma_0^2$

$\chi^2_{(\alpha)} = 2.70$ (from Table 5-12)

Solve for χ^2:

$$\chi^2 = (9)\frac{39.69}{30.25} = 11.81$$

Since $\chi^2 > \chi_{(a)}^2$, we reject H_0. The process standard deviation has increased.

-TEST

he F-test is used to compare two different sample variances.

The formula for the F-test is:

$$F = \frac{s_1^2}{s_2^2}$$

/here:

$_1^2 > s_2^2$

is the test statistic

$_1^2$ is sample variance 1

$_2^2$ is sample variance 2

xample: Two separate filling machines were sampled. lachine 1 variance is 0.50 ounces (n=10) and Machine 2 ariance is 0.95 ounces (n = 15). Is there a difference in ariance between these two machines (use $\alpha = 0.05$)?

$H_0: \sigma_1^2 = \sigma_2{}^2{}_0$

$H_a: \sigma_1^2 > \sigma_2{}^2{}_0$

$F_{(\alpha)} = 2.24$ (from Table 5-13)

Solve for F:

$$F = \frac{0.95}{0.50} = 1.9$$

Since $F > F_{(\alpha)}$, we reject H_0. The variance of Machine 2 is arger than that of Machine 1.

COMMON VALUES FOR THE χ^2 DISTRIBUTION

	α				α		
n	0.10	0.05	0.025	n	0.10	0.05	0.025
2	0.016	0.004	0.001	20	11.651	10.117	8.907
3	0.211	0.103	0.051	21	12.443	10.851	9.591
4	0.584	0.352	0.216	22	13.240	11.591	10.283
5	1.064	0.711	0.484	23	14.041	12.338	10.982
6	1.610	1.145	0.831	24	14.848	13.091	11.689
7	2.204	1.635	1.237	25	15.659	13.848	12.401
8	2.833	2.167	1.690	26	16.473	14.611	13.120
9	3.490	2.733	2.180	27	17.292	15.379	13.844
10	4.168	3.325	2.700	28	18.114	16.151	14.573
11	4.865	3.940	3.247	29	18.939	16.928	15.308
12	5.578	4.575	3.816	30	19.768	17.708	16.047
13	6.304	5.226	4.404	40	28.196	25.695	23.654
14	7.041	5.892	5.009	50	36.818	33.930	31.555
15	7.790	6.571	5.629	60	45.577	42.339	39.662
16	8.547	7.261	6.262	70	54.438	50.879	47.924
17	9.312	7.962	6.908	80	63.380	59.522	56.309
18	10.085	8.672	7.564	90	72.387	68.249	64.793
19	10.865	9.390	8.231	100	81.449	77.046	73.361

Table 5-12[a].

a. **Note:** Tables 5-4, 5-12 and 5-13 employ sample size (n) rather than the traditional degrees of freedom.

VALUES OF THE F DISTRIBUTION FOR $\alpha = 0.05$

$\alpha = 0.05$

n1 ▶ n2 ▼	2	3	4	5	6	7	8	9	10
2	161.45	199.50	215.71	224.58	230.16	233.99	236.77	238.88	240.54
3	18.51	19.00	19.16	19.25	19.30	19.33	19.35	19.37	19.38
4	10.13	9.55	9.28	9.12	9.01	8.94	8.89	8.85	8.81
5	7.71	6.94	6.59	6.39	6.26	6.16	6.09	6.04	6.00
6	6.61	5.79	5.41	5.19	5.05	4.95	4.88	4.82	4.77
7	5.99	5.14	4.76	4.53	4.39	4.28	4.21	4.15	4.10
8	5.59	4.74	4.35	4.12	3.97	3.87	3.79	3.73	3.68
9	5.32	4.46	4.07	3.84	3.69	3.58	3.50	3.44	3.39
10	5.12	4.26	3.86	3.63	3.48	3.37	3.29	3.23	3.18
15	4.54	3.68	3.29	3.06	2.90	2.79	2.71	2.64	2.59
20	4.38	3.52	3.13	2.90	2.74	2.63	2.54	2.48	2.42
25	4.26	3.40	3.01	2.78	2.62	2.51	2.42	2.36	2.30
30	4.18	3.33	2.93	2.70	2.55	2.43	2.35	2.28	2.22
40	4.09	3.24	2.85	2.61	2.46	2.34	2.26	2.19	2.13
50	4.04	3.19	2.79	2.56	2.40	2.29	2.20	2.13	2.08

Table 5-13a. (Continued on next page)

VALUES OF THE F DISTRIBUTION FOR $\alpha = 0.05$

$\alpha = 0.05$

n2 ▼ / n1 ▶	2	3	4	5	6	7	8	9	10
60	4.00	3.15	2.76	2.53	2.37	2.26	2.17	2.10	2.04
100	3.94	3.09	2.70	2.46	2.31	2.19	2.10	2.03	1.98
120	3.92	3.07	2.68	2.45	2.29	2.18	2.09	2.02	1.96
∞	3.84	3.00	2.61	2.37	2.22	2.10	2.01	1.94	1.88

$\alpha = 0.05$

n2 ▼ / n1 ▶	15	20	30	40	50	60	100	120	∞
2	245.36	247.69	249.95	251.06	251.72	252.16	253.03	253.25	254.29
3	19.42	19.44	19.46	19.47	19.48	19.48	19.49	19.49	19.50
4	8.71	8.67	8.62	8.60	8.58	8.57	8.55	8.55	8.53
5	5.87	5.81	5.75	5.72	5.70	5.69	5.66	5.66	5.63
6	4.64	4.57	4.50	4.47	4.45	4.43	4.41	4.40	4.37
7	3.96	3.88	3.81	3.78	3.76	3.74	3.71	3.70	3.67
8	3.53	3.46	3.38	3.34	3.32	3.31	3.28	3.27	3.23
9	3.24	3.16	3.08	3.05	3.02	3.01	2.98	2.97	2.93
10	3.03	2.95	2.87	2.83	2.80	2.79	2.76	2.75	2.71

Table 5-13a. (Continued on next page)

VALUES OF THE F DISTRIBUTION FOR $\alpha = 0.05$

n1 ▲ / n2 ▼	15	20	30	40	50	60	100	120	∞
					$\alpha = 0.05$				
15	2.42	2.34	2.25	2.21	2.18	2.16	2.12	2.11	2.07
20	2.26	2.17	2.08	2.03	2.00	1.98	1.94	1.93	1.88
25	2.13	2.04	1.95	1.90	1.86	1.84	1.80	1.79	1.73
30	2.05	1.96	1.86	1.81	1.78	1.76	1.71	1.70	1.64
40	1.95	1.86	1.76	1.70	1.67	1.65	1.60	1.59	1.52
50	1.90	1.80	1.70	1.64	1.61	1.58	1.53	1.52	1.45
60	1.86	1.77	1.66	1.60	1.57	1.54	1.49	1.47	1.40
100	1.79	1.69	1.58	1.52	1.48	1.45	1.39	1.38	1.29
120	1.78	1.67	1.56	1.50	1.46	1.43	1.37	1.35	1.26
∞	1.69	1.59	1.47	1.40	1.36	1.32	1.25	1.23	1.05

able 5-13a. (Continued)

How to Perform Hypothesis Testing

1. Define test values for null and alternate hypotheses.
2. Specify as a one-tail or two-tail test.
3. Specify the significance level (α).
4. Determine the sample size.
5. Select a random sample.
6. Select the appropriate hypothesis test:
   a. *Z-test:* compare sample average to a standard value, standard deviation known.
   b. *Two-Sample Z-test:* compare the means of two independent populations, standard deviations known.
   c. *Paired Z-test:* compare the means of two non-independent populations, standard deviations known.
   d. *t-test:* compare sample average to a standard value, standard deviation unknown.
   e. *Two-Sample t-test:* compare the means of two independent populations, standard deviations known.
   f. *Paired t-test:* compare the means of two non-independent populations, standard deviations known.
   g. *Single Proportion Test:* compare a binomial proportion to a specified value.
   h. *Two-Sample Proportion Test:* binomial comparison of two samples.
   i. *χ^2 Test:* compare a sample variance to a specified value.
   j. *F-test:* compare two different sample variances.
7. Perform the analysis and interpret results.
8. If $p < \alpha$, reject null hypothesis.

CHAPTER SIX
Control Charts

What Are Control Charts?

Control charts are specialized graphs that provide us with information in two dimensions: the distribution of the process (average and variance) and process trending. Figure 6-1 is an example of a typical control chart. Control charts possess the following attributes:

1. *Center line:* represents the average value (measurement or proportion) of a specified characteristic.
2. *Upper control limit (UCL):* a boundary that is three units of standard deviation above the center line.
3. *Lower control limit (LCL):* a boundary that is three units of standard deviation (with some exceptions) below the center line.

GENERIC CONTROL CHART

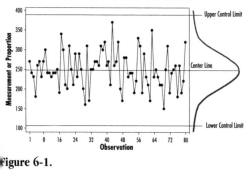

Figure 6-1.

Application of Control Charts in Six Sigma

In *Six Sigma*, control charts are used to baseline process performance, monitor and control process performance, evaluate measurement systems, compare multiple processes, compare processes before and after a change, etc. Control charts can be used in virtually any situation that relates to process characterization and analysis.

How to Use Control Charts

Sample data (also called *subgroup* data) is plotted on a control chart to monitor process stability. In a stable process, sample observations will be randomly distributed around the center line of the control chart. This random arrangement of data reflects the normal variation that we would expect in any process (*common cause variation*). When the data pattern is not random, it's a signal that a process shift has occurred and the process is unstable (*special cause variation*).

If a *special cause signal* occurs, the process should be studied to determine the cause of the signal. If an assignable cause for the problem is identified, appropriate action should be taken to correct it.

Special Cause Signals: the following events signal a potential special cause (note: all eight events apply to variables control charts. When using attributes control charts, only events 1, 4, 7, and 8 apply):

1. An observation occurring more than 3 units of standard deviation from the center line, i.e., any points occurring outside of the lower or upper control limits.

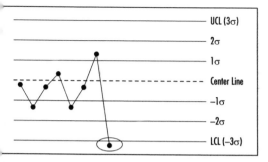

2. Two out of three consecutive observations (all on the same side of the center line) occurring more than 2 units of standard deviation away from the center line.

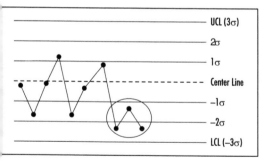

3. Four out of five consecutive observations (all on the same side of the center line) occurring more than 1 unit of standard deviation away from the center line.

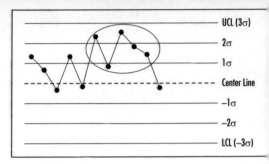

4. Eight consecutive observations occurring on one side of the center line.

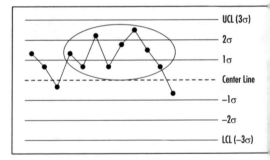

5. Fifteen consecutive observations occurring within 1 unit of standard deviation from the center line.

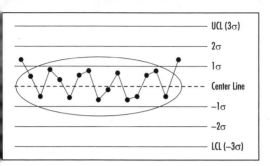

6. Eight consecutive observations that are more than 1 unit of standard deviation from the center line.

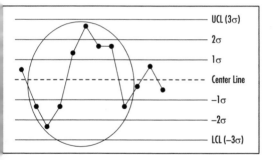

7. Fourteen consecutive observations that alternate up and down.

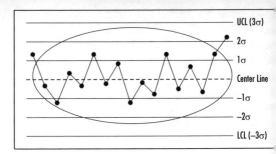

8. Six consecutive observations that trend downward or upward.

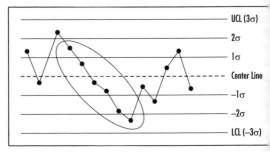

Rational Subgroups

A rational subgroup is a sample where all items included in the sample were produced under very similar conditions. The selection of rational subgroups is performed in such a way as to include only common cause variation within each of the sample subgroups. A special cause signal will occur when the variation between subgroups is significantly greater than the variation within subgroups. The selection of good rational subgroups is important in enabling us to distinguish a signal (*special cause variation*) from the process noise (*common cause variation*). Also, rational subgroup sizes are usually small; we typically select a constant sample size of 2-5 units.

When applying control charts to detect process shifts, rational subgroups usually consist of units that were produced as closely together as possible. An example of a rational sub-group is a sample that consists of 4 consecutive bottles from a filling machine that fills 50 bottles per minute.

When dealing with multiple operators, multiple cavity molds, multiple spindle machines, and other processes that produce multiple streams of output it may be advised to use separate control charts for each of the output streams.

Control Charts for Discrete (Attribute) Data

Attribute control charts are used with proportion and count data. Typically, attribute control charts are used to display and track proportions or counts for some characteristic of interest (e.g, proportion of nonconforming product, the number of customers served, etc).

P Chart

The p chart is used when it is desired to monitor the proportion of items that possess a specific characteristic. P charts are commonly used to graph the proportion of nonconforming products or transactions. When using samples of different size, the upper and lower control limits of a p chart will be uneven (refer to Figure 6-2). P charts are used when sample subgroup sizes are either equal or unequal.

The characteristics of the *p* chart are:

1. Center Line: the average of the sample *p* values; symbol is $\bar{p}$.
2. Upper Control Limit:
$$\bar{p} + 3 \sqrt{\frac{\bar{p}(1-\bar{p})}{n}}$$
3. Lower Control Limit*:
$$\bar{p} - 3 \sqrt{\frac{\bar{p}(1-\bar{p})}{n}}$$

*When the calculated value for the lower control limit is a negative number, a lower control limit is not placed on the control chart.

where:
n is the number of samples (subgroups)

Example: A medical device company inspects purchased material before releasing it to the production floor. An abbreviated list of the inspection results for the last 78 shipments is shown in Table 6-1. Construct a p control chart for the proportion of defective material.

INSPECTION RECORD (N = 78)

Units Sampled	Units Defective
989	59
1009	57
988	47
946	52
1078	47
1004	48
980	46
1028	56
—	—
—	—
—	—
1094	44

Table 6-1.

The p chart (Figure 6-2) shows that the average level of proportion defective material supplied to the medical company is 0.00374 ($\bar{p}$) and that the normal range for the proportion of defective material received is 0.00000 (LCL) to approximately 0.00953 (UCL). The process appears to be stable, since all plotted sample values occur inside of the upper and lower control limit boundaries. Note that the control limits are uneven, due to the unequal number of units sampled.

P CONTROL CHART

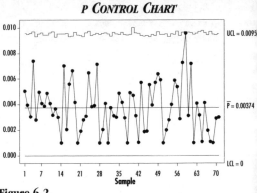

Figure 6-2.

NP CHART

The *np* chart is similar to the *p* chart except that it displays the number (rather than proportion) of items that possess a specific characteristic (e.g., amount of nonconforming product). The np chart is used when subgroup sample sizes are equal.

The characteristics of the np chart are:

1. Center Line: $n\bar{p}$
2. Upper Control Limit: $n\bar{p} + 3\sqrt{n\bar{p}(1-\bar{p})}$
3. Lower Control Limit*: $n\bar{p} - 3\sqrt{n\bar{p}(1-\bar{p})}$

* When the calculated value for the lower control limit is a negative number, a lower control limit is not placed on the control chart.

Example: An np control chart was constructed using a subgroup sample size of 1,000 units.

The *np* chart (Figure 6-3) shows that the process is stable and the average amount of defective material supplied to the medical company is 3.75 units (np) and that the normal range for amount of defective material received is 0.00 (LCL) to 9.54 (UCL) units.

NP CONTROL CHART

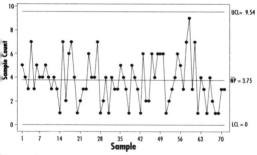

Figure 6-3.

C CHART

The *c* chart is used to track the number of defects per unit of measurement, with a sample unit of constant size (area of opportunity is the same for every subgroup) and the probability of a defect occurring in a specific location is low. The *c* control chart is appropriate whenever it is desired to count more than one defect per sample unit, e.g., the number of flaws in a square meter of carpet classified as dirt, tears, and voids.

The characteristics of the c chart are:

1. Center Line: the average of the subgroup defects; symbol is $\bar{c}$.

2. Upper Control Limit: $\bar{c} + 3\sqrt{\bar{c}}$

3. Lower Control Limit*: $\bar{c} - 3\sqrt{\bar{c}}$

* When the calculated value for the lower control limit is a negative number, a lower control limit is not placed on the control chart.

Example: A bank randomly samples a loan approval worksheet used by its staff. The worksheet has a large number of items that are required to be completed by the staff. Table 6-2 shows the counts of incomplete items per worksheet (each worksheet is a subgroup) for a sample of n = 98. Construct a c chart to evaluate the bank employees' performance.

COUNTS OF INCOMPLETE ITEMS

Incomplete Items Per Worksheet						
4	5	3	2	2	2	2
4	5	5	4	3	2	6
4	2	2	1	4	3	4
1	1	4	4	3	5	3
3	6	5	2	7	7	3
6	3	6	5	4	4	3
3	5	5	6	8	5	4
4	4	2	2	2	1	4
2	2	4	1	1	4	5
3	6	7	4	7	2	3
2	6	2	10	7	6	2
8	2	3	5	6	4	6
4	1	7	2	6	4	7
6	5	4	7	2	2	5

Table 6-2.

The *c* chart (Figure 6-4) shows that the average for incomplete items is 3.99 ($\bar{c}$) and that the normal range for the incomplete items is 0.00 (LCL) to 9.98 (UCL). One sample falls beyond the UCL, indicating the presence of a special cause. An investigation into the special cause revealed that the volume of applications was much higher on the day that the special cause signal occurred and the staff was cutting corners to deal with the increased customer volume.

c CONTROL CHART

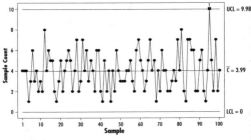

Figure 6-4.

u CHART

The u chart is similar to the c chart, except that the sample unit is not required to have a constant size (area of opportunity need not be constant).

The characteristics of the u chart are:

1. *Center Line:* the total number of occurrences in the sample (subgroup) divided by the total opportunity area; symbol is $\bar{u}$.

2. *Upper Control Limit:* $\bar{u} + 3 \sqrt{\dfrac{\bar{u}}{n}}$

3. Lower Control Limit: $\bar{u} - 3\sqrt{\dfrac{\bar{u}}{n}}$

*When the calculated value for the lower control limit is a negative number, a lower control limit is not placed on the control chart.

Example: A furniture manufacturer inspects its products for surface finish defects and the surface area inspected depends on the type of product sampled. Table 6-3 is a partial listing of finish defects and area inspected. Construct a u chart to assess process stability.

The u chart (Figure 6-5) shows that the average occurrence of finish defects per unit is 0.0590 ($\bar{u}$) and that the normal range for finish defects is 0.0000 (LCL) to 0.1319 (UCL). Two samples have values beyond the UCL, indicating process instability and the presence of special causes. An investigation revealed that a new, inexperienced operator was the source of a higher than normal number of defects per unit.

SURFACE FINISH DEFECTS

Finish Defects	Area Inspected
3	130
13	140
7	140
6	140
4	130

Table 6-3. (Continued on next page)

SURFACE FINISH DEFECTS

Finish Defects	Area Inspected
15	110
5	110
—	—
—	—
—	—
4	100

Table 6-3. (Continued)

u CONTROL CHART

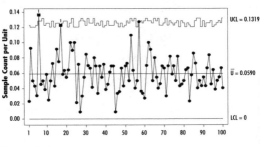

Figure 6-5.

Control Charts for Continuous Data

Variables control charts are used with continuous (measurement) data and are normally used to monitor and control the inputs (x variables) that affect process performance. Some examples of measurable characteristics used with variables control charts are: length, volume, speed, temperature, etc.

INDIVIDUALS CHART

The *individuals* chart is used when it isn't reasonable to use sample subgroups (see section on rational subgroups) or in situations where data is generated slowly. Individuals charts work best when used with data that is *normally distributed* (non-normal data should be transformed to normal).

The characteristics of the *individuals* chart are:

1. Center Line: the average of the individual observations; symbol is $\bar{x}$.

2. Upper Control Limit: $\bar{x} + 3\sigma$

3. Lower Control Limit: $\bar{x} - 3\sigma$

Example: The manager of a customer service center is interested in improving customer satisfaction by reducing telephone hold time. He decides to use an individuals chart to assess hold time stability and prepares the individuals chart shown in Figure 6-6.

The individuals chart shows that telephone hold time is stable. The average hold time is 248.4 seconds ($\bar{x}$) and the normal range for hold time is 106.6 seconds (LCL) to 390.1 seconds (UCL).

INDIVIDUALS CONTROL CHART

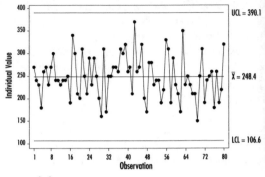

Figure 6-6.

MOVING RANGE (MR) CHART

Moving range charts are usually used in conjunction with individuals charts to monitor process variation stability. Moving range values are calculated by taking the difference between successive pairs of measurements.

The characteristics of the *MR* chart are:

1. Center Line: the average of the moving ranges; symbol is $\overline{MR}$.

2. Upper Control Limit: $\overline{MR} \cdot 3.267$

3. Lower Control Limit: none

Example: An *MR* control chart for the customer service center is shown in Figure 6-7. Is the hold time variability stable?

MOVING RANGE CHART

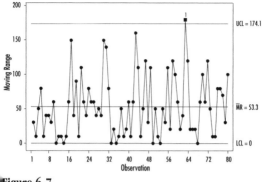

Figure 6-7.

The MR chart shows an average for the moving range equal to 53.3 seconds ($\overline{MR}$). The normal values for MR are expected to fall between 0.0 seconds (LCL) and 174.1 seconds (UCL). The one point that is outside of the upper control limit was caused by the malfunction of telephone switching equipment.

RANGE (R) CHART

The range chart is used to monitor process variation stability. R values measure the variation within sample subgroups. The R control chart is normally used in conjunction with the $\overline{x}$ chart.

The characteristics of the R chart are:

1. Center Line: the average of the subgroup ranges; symbol is $\overline{R}$.

2. Upper Control Limit: ($\bar{R}$) (D4)

3. Lower Control Limit: ($\bar{R}$) (D3)

Note: See Table 6-4 (Table of Constants for $\bar{x}$ and R Charts) for D3 and D4 values.

Example: A quality engineer for a metal machining company prepared an R chart (subgroup size = 3) to assess process variation stability of electrode diameter for a product used in the electroplating industry. Comment on her control chart (Figure 6-8).

The R chart shows the variability to be stable, since none of the subgroup ranges fall outside of the control limits. The average range for electrode diameter is 0.3169 cm ($\bar{R}$) and the normal process width for diameter range is 0.0000 cm (LCL) to 0.8157 cm (UCL).

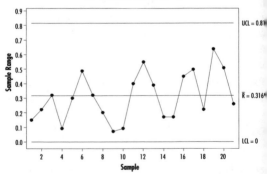

R CONTROL CHART

Figure 6-8.

$\bar{x}$ Chart

The $\bar{x}$ chart is used to monitor the stability of the process mean. Averages of sample subgroups are plotted on the control chart to provide a display of subgroup-to-subgroup variation. $\bar{x}$ charts are typically used in moderate to high volume production environments where it makes sense to use sample subgroups.

The characteristics of the $\bar{x}$ chart are:

1. Center Line: the average of subgroup (sample) averages, symbol is $\bar{\bar{x}}$.

2. Upper Control Limit: $\bar{\bar{x}} + (\bar{R})(A_2)$

3. Lower Control Limit: $\bar{\bar{x}} - (\bar{R})(A_2)$

Note: See Table 6-4 (Table of Constants for $\bar{x}$ and R Charts) for values of A_2.

Example: After assessing the within subgroup variation using an R chart, the quality engineer produced an $\bar{x}$ chart to check the subgroup-to-subgroup variability (Figure 6-9).

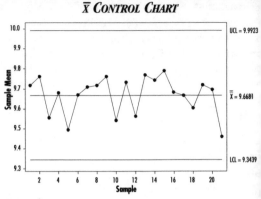

$\overline{X}$ Control Chart

Figure 6-9.

The $\overline{x}$ chart shows the process average to be stable, since none of the subgroup averages fall outside of the control limits. The average of the subgroup averages for electrode diameter is 9.6681 cm (x) and the normal range for average diameter is between 9.3439 cm (LCL) and 9.9923 cm (UCL).

Table of Constants for $\overline{X}$ and R Charts

n	A_2	D_3	D_4
2	1.880	0.000	3.267
3	1.023	0.000	2.574
4	0.729	0.000	2.282
5	0.577	0.000	2.114

Table 6-4. (Continued on next page)

TABLE OF CONSTANTS FOR $\bar{x}$ AND R CHARTS

n	A_2	D_3	D_4
6	0.483	0.000	2.004
7	0.419	0.076	1.924
8	0.373	0.136	1.864
9	0.337	0.184	1.816
10	0.308	0.223	1.777

Table 6-4. (Continued)

EWMA CHART

The EWMA (exponentially weighted moving average) chart is used when it is desired to detect small process shifts. The formula used to calculate the exponentially weighted moving average is:

$$z_{(t)} = \lambda \bar{x}_t + (1 + \lambda)\, z_{(t-1)}$$

where:

$z_{(t)}$ is the weighted average for all samples prior to time period "t"

λ is a weighting constant whose value is between o and 1 (smaller values will detect smaller process shifts)

$\bar{x}_t$ is the sample (subgroup) average

$z_{(t-1)}$ is the weighted average for time period prior to time t; i.e., $t - 1$

The formulas for calculating the upper and lower control limits are:

$$UCL = \overline{\overline{X}} + 3\sigma \sqrt{\frac{\lambda}{(2-\lambda)n}}$$

$$LCL = \overline{\overline{X}} - 3\sigma \sqrt{\frac{\lambda}{(2-\lambda)n}}$$

Example: Table 6-5 shows the subgroup averages of the data from the electrode diameter example and the $z_{(t)}$ values that were calculated with them, using a subgroup size of 3. The value of z_0 is used in the calculation of the initial EWMA value (z_1) and is the grand average of the subgroup averages. Here, z_0 is equal to 9.6681 cm, as shown in Figure 6-9.

$Z_{(T)}$ VALUES

Sample	$X_{(t)}$	$Z_{(t)}$
1	9.7167	9.6778
2	9.7600	9.6943
3	9.5533	9.6661
4	9.6800	9.6689
5	9.4933	9.6337
6	9.6700	9.6410
7	9.7100	9.6548
8	9.7167	9.6672
9	9.7600	9.6857

Table 6-5. (Continued on next page)

$Z_{(T)}$ VALUES

Sample	$X_{(t)}$	$Z_{(t)}$
10	9.6633	9.6813
11	9.7133	9.6877
12	9.7167	9.6535
13	9.7033	9.6954
14	9.7567	9.7077
15	9.6933	9.7048
16	9.6667	9.6972
17	9.6267	9.6831
18	9.6133	9.6691
19	9.7467	9.6846

Table 6-5. (Continued)

The EWMA chart that was generated from the electrode diameter data is shown in Figure 6-10. When using statistical software to create an EWMA control chart, all that is required is your raw data, the subgroup size, and a value for λ.

The EWMA control chart should be used in situations where it is necessary to detect small shifts in process average. Using lower λ values makes the EWMA control chart more sensitive (as λ decreases, sensitivity increases) and will allow you to detect smaller process shifts.

EWMA Control Chart

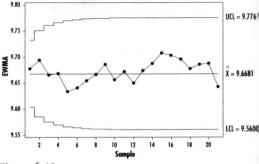

Figure 6-10.

How to Create and Use Control Charts

1. Specify the characteristics that you are interested in control charting.

2. Specify the type of data that will be used:
   a. Discrete: counts, proportions, percentages.
   b. Continuous: all measurement data, e.g., length, volume, speed, etc.

3. Define the sampling approach:
   a. Determine rational subgroups, if necessary.
   b. Specify sample size.
   c. Specify sampling frequency.

4. Select the appropriate control chart:
   a. p Chart: use to plot the proportion or percentage of defects.

b. np Chart: similar to p chart; use to plot the number of defects (discrete data).

c. c Chart: use to plot the number of defects per unit that occur within a constant area of opportunity (discrete data).

d. u Chart: similar to c chart; use to plot the average number of defects per unit when the area of opportunity is not constant (discrete data).

e. Individuals Chart: use to plot individual measurements (continuous data).

f. Moving Range (MR) Chart: use to plot process variability when working with individual measurements (continuous data).

g. Range (R) Chart: use to plot process variability when working with sample subgroups (continuous data).

h. $\bar{x}$ Chart: use to plot the process average of sample subgroups (continuous data).

i. Exponentially Weighted Moving Average (EWMA) Chart: use as an alternative to the $\bar{x}$ chart when it is desired to detect small process shifts (continuous data).

5. Begin sampling and charting data on a run chart. Plot the data on the control chart when there is a sufficient number of individual values or subgroups:

a. Attribute control charts: 25 or more.

b. Variables control charts: 50 or more.

6. Monitor the control chart for process stability. If a special cause signal occurs, take corrective action as required.

7. Upper and lower control limits should be recalculated whenever a significant change in the process is implemented that alters the output of the process.

CHAPTER SEVEN
Correlation Analysis

What Is Correlation Analysis?

Correlation analysis is a method that is used to measure the strength of the linear relationship between two or more continuous variables.

Application of Correlation Analysis in Six Sigma

In *Six Sigma*, correlation analysis is applied to identify the key process input variables, i.e., the vital few input variables that have the greatest effect on process output and product or service quality.

Scatter Plots

Scatter plots are used to graphically depict correlation between single Y and X variables. Figure 7-1 is an example of a scatter plot used to show the correlation between the percent yield of a chemical process and the temperature of the solution in the chemical reaction. The plot shows a definite linear pattern; the process yield is increasing as the solution temperature becomes higher.

Correlation Matrix

The correlation matrix (Table 7-1) calculates a *correlation coefficient* for all combinations of variables under evaluation. The *correlation coefficient*, commonly referred to as r, is a statistical measure of the strength of the linear relation-

SCATTER PLOT

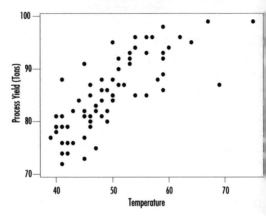

Figure 7-1.

ship between two variables. The value of r ranges from −1.00 to +1.00. A perfect correlation is indicated by a value of 1.00 (either positive or negative). A value of zero indicates that no correlation is present.

To use the *correlation matrix*, read down any column to get the r-value that corresponds with the row variable. For example, the r-value for X_1 with X_2 is 0.82, X_3 with X_4 is -1.00, X_5 with X_6 is -0.24, etc.

CORRELATION MATRIX

Variables	X_1	X_2	X_3	X_4	X_5
X_2	0.82	—	—	—	—
X_3	−1.00	−0.82	—	—	—
X_4	1.00	0.82	−1.00	—	—
X_5	−0.82	−1.00	0.82	−0.82	—
X_6	0.39	0.24	−0.39	0.39	−0.24

Table 7-1.

Figure 7-2 shows examples of scatter plots with their corresponding r-values. This helps us to visualize different degrees of correlation between two variables.

SCATTER PLOTS AND CORRESPONDING R-VALUES

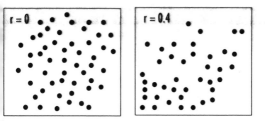

Figure 7-2. (Continued on next page)

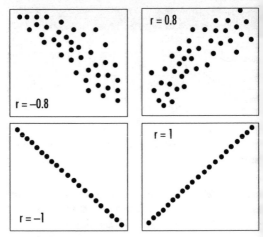

Figure 7-2. (Continued)

Example 1: You're working on a project to reduce the amount of time that it takes to deliver your products, i.e., the elapsed time from initiation of the order to the time the customer actually receives the product. You decide to use correlation analysis and prepare the matrix shown in Table 7-2.

The correlation matrix exhibits relatively high r-values for the linear relationships between *Order Entry Time* (0.743) and *Total Time* (0.890). Also, *Warehouse Picking Time* and *Packing Time* have a very high r-value (0.943). Since it appears that *Order Entry* has a moderate to strong linear

CORRELATION MATRIX FOR DELIVERY TIME

Variables	Order Entry Time	Warehouse Picking Time	Packing Time	Inspection Time
Warehouse Picking Time	0.743	—	—	—
Packing Time	−0.057	−0.076	—	—
Inspection Time	0.490	0.523	−0.066	—
Total Time	0.890	0.591	−0.067	0.492

Table 7-2.

relationship with all of the process variables, with the exception of Packing Time, your next step would be to investigate the Order Entry process for improvement opportunities.

SIGNIFICANCE OF THE CORRELATION ANALYSIS

Sample size has a major effect on the significance of the estimated value of r. The greater the sample size, the better will be the estimate of r. To ensure that we make the proper decisions when using correlation analysis, we must test the significance of each r-value that is estimated.

To determine if the r-value is significant, we estimate a p-value. If the p-value is less than the desired significance level, we can be confident that there really is a relationship between the variables. For example, if we choose a 95% confidence level for our correlation analysis, our significance level is 0.05 (1 − confidence level = significance level).

Using Minitab, we can estimate both r-values and their corresponding p-values, as shown in Table 7-3.

CORRELATION MATRIX WITH P-VALUES

Variables	Order Entry Time	Warehouse Picking Time	Packing Time	Inspection Time
Warehouse Picking Time	0.743	—	—	—
p-value	0.000	—	—	—
Packing Time	−0.057	−0.076	—	—
p-value	0.487	0.358	—	—
Inspection Time	0.490	0.523	−0.066	—
p-value	0.000	0.000	0.423	—
Total Time	0.890	0.591	−0.067	0.492
p-value	0.000	0.000	0.413	0.000

Table 7-3.

Example 2: From Example 1, was our conclusion correct that *Order Entry Time*, *Warehouse Picking Time*, *Inspection Time*, and *Total Time* are correlated at the 0.05 significance level?

Yes. The p-values for all of those variables is zero, which is less than our 0.05 significance level.

How to Perform Correlation Analysis

1. Estimate sample size.
2. Generate a scatter plot (two-variables) or a correlation matrix (two or more variables).
3. When using a scatter plot, look to see if the plotted points align in a linear or non-linear pattern. If so, correlation is evident.
4. When using a correlation matrix, evaluate the r-values and their related p-values. If the p-value is less than the significance level (usually set equal to 0.05), linear correlation is evident.
5. Be aware of non-linear correlation. When a non-linear relationship exists between two variables, the correlation matrix will not show it. For example, Figure 7-3 shows a situation where the r-value for X_2 and Y_2 is 0.002 (no linear relationship). However, the scatter plot's pattern shows a strong quadratic relationship between X_2 and Y_2.

EXAMPLE: STRONG NON-LINEAR RELATIONSHIP (R-VALUE IS 0.002)

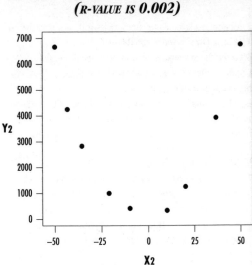

Figure 7-3.

CHAPTER EIGHT
Regression Analysis

What Is Regression Analysis?

Regression analysis is an approach that is used to define the mathematical relationship between an output variable (y) and one or more input variables (x). This mathematical relationship is expressed in the form of a regression model, which is used to predict the value of the output variable as a function of the value of the input variables.

Application of Regression Analysis in Six Sigma

In Six Sigma, regression analysis is used to:

1. Predict the output level of a process, e.g., process yield, product defects, etc.
2. Determine the mathematical relationship between process inputs and process outputs. Examples are: the effect of temperature (input) on the weight of a molded plastic part (output) and the effect of labor hours and utility costs (inputs) on the price of a product or service (output).
3. Predict resource requirements to satisfy business needs, e.g., the number of call center staff required to service customers at varying levels of customer demand, the number of maintenance technicians required to support manufacturing operations, etc.
4. Predict product or service cycle time, e.g., the amount of time required to fulfill customer delivery requirements

for customized products, the number of customer services representatives required to quickly respond to customer inquiries, etc.

Simple Linear Regression

Simple linear regression is used to determine the mathematical relationship between a single input variable (x) and an output variable (y).

The mathematical model for simple linear regression is:

$$\hat{Y}_i = b_0 + b_1 x_i + e_i$$

where:

$\hat{Y}_i$ is the predicted value of the output variable

b_0 is the y-intercept (value of y when x = 0)

b_1 is the slope (the rate of change in y for each unit change in x)

x_i is the value of the input variable

e_i is the residual value; a measurement of the difference between the original y-value and the y-value predicted by the regression model (refer to Figure 8-1).

REGRESSION MODEL COMPONENTS

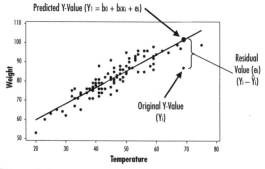

Figure 8-1.

Example: A customer call center at a large bank desires to maintain their call abandonment rate (the proportion of customers who hang-up without having spoken to a customer service associate) at 0.08 or less. A relationship exists between the abandonment rate and the number of customer service associates available in the call center, as shown by a scatter plot (see Figure 8-2). Using simple linear regression, define the mathematical relationship between the abandonment rate and the number of customer service associates available to answer calls. What is the average number of customer service associates that the bank must have available in the call center to achieve their service goal?

Using simple linear regression, we determine the regression equation for predicting the abandonment rate (Table 8-1).

CALL ABANDONMENT SCATTER PLOT

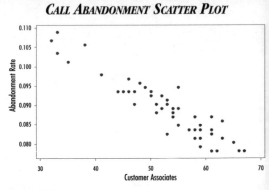

Figure 8-2.

Table 8-2 is a partial listing of the original data, with estimates of the fitted y-values (calculated using the regression equation) and their corresponding residuals.

REGRESSION ANALYSIS OUTPUT

Regression Analysis: abandonment rate versus customer associates				
The regression equation is Abandonment Rate = 0.131 − 0.0001 Customer Associates				
Predictor	Coef	SE Coef	T	P
Constant	0.131	0.00207	63.44	0.000
Customer Associates	−0.001	0.00004	−21.03	0.000
$S = 0.00264473$ $R - Sq = 85.7\%$				

Table 8-1.

CALL CENTER DATA AND ESTIMATES

Customer Associates X_i	Abandonment Rate Y_i	Predicted Y-Value $\hat{Y}_i$	Residual $Y_i - \hat{Y}_i = e_i$
53	0.083	0.089	−0.006
38	0.106	0.101	0.005
47	0.094	0.094	0.000
—	—	—	—
—	—	—	—
—	—	—	—
53	0.091	0.089	0.002

Table 8-2.

Figure 8-3 is a plot of the regression line (predicted y-values) superimposed on a scatter plot of the original y-values.

REGRESSION (PREDICTED Y) PLOT

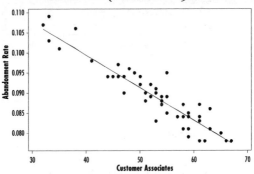

Figure 8-3.

In order to determine the average number of customer service associates required, we rearrange the regression equation and solve for x:

Regression Equation:

abandonment rate =

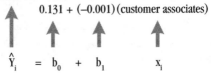

$$\hat{Y}_i = b_0 + b_1 \qquad x_i$$

0.131 + (−0.001)(customer associates)

Solve Equation for X:

$$\frac{\hat{Y}_i - b_0}{b_1} = x_i \implies \frac{0.08 - 0.131}{-0.001} = 51$$

Our model predicts that at least 51 customer service asso-ciates must be available to answer calls, in order to maintain a customer abandonment rate of 0.08 or less.

How to Interpret Regression Analysis Results

Table 8-3 (next page) illustrates the computer output from the call center example. Let's take a look at each of the table entries and how to interpret them.

1. *Regression equation:* this is the regression model itself ($\hat{y} = 0.131 - 0.0001\, x$); where $\hat{y}$ is the predicted *aban-donment rate* and x is the number of *customer associates*.

2. *Predictor:* this is a description of the factors in the regression model. *Constant* refers to b_0 (the y-intercept) and *customer associates* is the name of the x-variable that was used in the model.

3. *Coef:* these are the values of the coefficients b_0 and b_1.

4. *SE Coef:* these are the estimates of the standard deviation for b_0 and b_1 that are used in the t-tests of b_0 and b_1 (see T and P below).

5. *T:* these are the t-values of the regression coefficients. Large t-values suggest that the coefficients are statistically significant (see P below).

6. *P:* these are the p-values for the regression coefficients.

REGRESSION ANALYSIS OUTPUT

Regression Analysis: abandonment rate versus customer associates

The regression eqution is
Abandonment Rate = 0.131 − 0.0001 Customer Associates   **1**

	2	**3**	**4**	**5**	**6**
Predictor	Coef	SE Coef	T	P
Constant	0.131	0.00207	63.44	0.000
Customer Associates	−0.001	0.00004	−21.03	0.000

7	**8**	
S = 0.00264473	R − Sq = 85.7%	

Table 8-3.

Generally, when P < 0.05, the regression coefficient is considered to be statistically significant (useful to predict Y).

7. *S:* this is the standard error of the estimate, which provides an estimate of the standard deviation for the regression equation, i.e., the variation of points around the regression line.

8. *R − Sq:* this is the r^2 value (coefficient of determination), which measures how useful the x-variable is in predicting the value of the y-variable. The value of r^2 ranges from zero (poor predictor) to one (excellent predictor).

Confidence and Prediction Intervals

In regression analysis, confidence and prediction intervals provide us with additional information regarding the prediction of y-values when using our model.

Confidence intervals are used to determine the range within which we would expect to find the average $\hat{Y}$-value for a specified x-value that was used in the regression model.

Example: Referring to Table 8-2, we see that when the number of customer associates (x) is 53, the predicted value for abandonment rate (y) is 0.089.

The confidence interval for the average abandonment rate with 53 customer associates is:

Fitted Y	SE Fit	95% CI
0.088801	0.000304	(0.088195, 0.089407)

Therefore, the average value of $\hat{Y}$ that occurs for x=53, will be contained within the interval of 0.088 to 0.089 (rounded), with 95% confidence.

Prediction intervals are used to determine the range within which we would expect to find a $\hat{Y}$-value for a specified x-value that was not included in the regression model.

Example: Determine the abandonment rate prediction interval for x=65:

Fitted Y	SE Fit	95% CI
0.079156	0.000530	(0.073781, 0.084530)

Therefore, the next value of $\hat{Y}$ that occurs when x=65, will be contained within the interval of 0.074 to 0.085 (rounded), with 95% confidence.

How Do We Know That Our Regression Model Is Good Enough to Use?

Our regression model will be used to predict the values for an output variable of interest, using a correlated input variable. Before using our model, we need to understand how effective it will be in helping us to estimate the values for our output variable. Two key measurements of model "goodness" are: r2 and p-value of the input (x) variable coefficient.

P-Value (X-Variable Coefficient)

The p-value measures the statistical significance of the input variable. It is generally accepted that if the p-value is less than 0.05, the input variable is significant, i.e., the input variable is useful in predicting the value of the output variable.

R² — Coefficient of Determination

A measure of how useful the x-variable is in predicting the value of the y-variable. The larger the r^2 value, the better the model. R² ranges from zero (poor model) to one (excellent model).

Example: Using the information from Table 8-3, determine if our model is useful for predicting call abandonment values.

Referring to Table 8-3, we see that the p-value associated with the coefficient of the number of customer service associates is much less than 0.05, providing very strong evidence that our input variable is appropriate to use in our model. In addition, r^2 is 85.7%. This means that almost 86% of the variation in the values that we observe for call abandonment rate (output variable) is explained by the number of customer service associates (input variable) available to answer customer calls.

Using Residual and Normal Probability Plots to Validate Regression Models

Before using our regression model, it is important that we validate it, using the criteria listed in Table 8-4. Figure 8-7 provides examples of residual plot patterns and how to interpret them.

MODEL VALIDATION CRITERIA

Validation Criterion	Diagnostic Tool	Action When Criterion Not Met
Residuals should be normally distributed	Normal probability plot or residual plots	Transform y or x and repeat regression analysis or perform non-linear regression
The variance of the residuals should be constant	Residual plots	Apply weighted regression analysis or transformation

Table 8-4.

Example: Using the model validation criteria (see Table 8-4), verify that the call center staffing model is appropriate to use.

1. Verify that the residuals are normally distributed, using a normal probability plot.
   The probability plot of the residuals (see Figure 8-4) shows that the residuals are approximately normally distributed. The model meets the normality criterion.

NORMAL PROBABILITY PLOT OF RESIDUALS

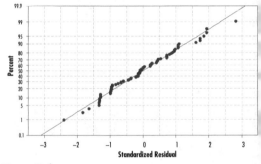

Figure 8-4.

2. Verify that the variance of the residuals is constant. Plot the residual values against the predicted y-values and the x-values (Figures 8-5 and 8-6).
   The plots of residuals against the predicted y-values (abandonment rate) and the x-values (number of customer associates) show that the residuals are randomly

distributed. The model meets the validation criterion for constant variance of the residuals. Having met both criteria, the model has been validated and is appropriate to use.

RESIDUALS VERSUS PREDICTED Y

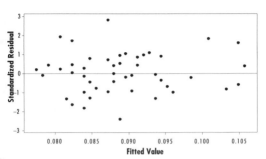

Figure 8-5.

RESIDUALS VERSUS X-VARIABLE

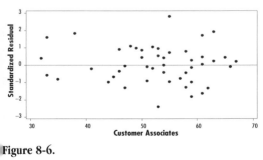

Figure 8-6.

Note: when only one x-variable is used in the regression model, the residual plots of the predicted y-values and the x-values are mirror images.

Interpreting Residual Plots

Figure 8-7 provides examples of patterns that occur with residual plots:

1. Figure 8-7A: Random
2. Figure 8-7B: Curvilinear
3. Figure 8-7C: Curvilinear and nonconstant variance
4. Figure 8-7D: Nonconstant variance

Multiple Regression

Multiple regression is an extension of simple linear regression and involves using two or more input variables (x) to predict the value of an output variable (y). The purpose of using several input variables is to improve the predictive capability of the regression model.

The mathematical model for multiple regression is:

$$\hat{Y}_i = b_0 + b_1 x_{i1} + b_2 x_{i2} + \ldots + b_n x_{in} + e_i$$

where:
$\hat{Y}_i$ is the fitted value of the output variable
b_0 is the y-intercept
b_n is the slope of the nth input variable
x_{in} is the value of the nth input variable
e_i is the residual value; a measurement of the difference between the original y-value and the y-value predicted by the regression model.

INTERPRETING RESIDUAL PLOTS

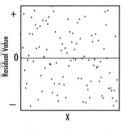

(A) Linear model is appropriate. No relationship exists between residuals and x-variable.

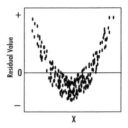

(B) Linear model is inappropriate. Curvilinear relationship exists between residuals and x-variable.

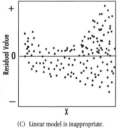

(C) Linear model is inappropriate. Variance of residuals is nonconstant and a curvilinear relationship exists between residuals and x-variable.

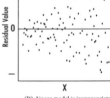

(D) Linear model is inappropriate. Variance of residuals is nonconstant

Figure 8-7.

Multicollinearity

Multicollinearity is a condition that occurs when a model's input variables are strongly correlated. Strongly correlated x-variables can affect the magnitude and sign of the regression coefficients and may mask an important x-variable by causing its p-value to appear insignificant. It's always a good practice to create a matrix plot or a correlation matrix to check for input variables that are highly correlated with one another. Also, when running a multiple regression analysis, it is prudent to generate *variance inflation factors* for the input variables and remove those that exceed the threshold for multicollinearity.

VARIANCE INFLATION FACTOR (VIF)

The VIF is a measure that is used to identify input variables that are strongly correlated. Multicollinearity is indicated whenever a VIF value is greater than 10. Input variables that have a VIF greater than 10 should be systematically removed from the model (we must also consider the p-values of the x-variables in the model to ensure that we don't eliminate variables that are highly significant).

SYSTEMATIC PROCEDURE FOR VIF > 10

1. Select the input variable with the highest VIF.
2. Use a matrix plot or correlation matrix to identify which of the other input variables are strongly correlated with the one under review.
3. Select the input variable that exhibits the strongest correlation with the one under review.
4. Look at the coefficients of the two input variables under

review. Check the signs of the coefficients to see if they make sense (e.g., a negative coefficient that should be positive). Remove the one that doesn't make sense and rerun the regression.

5. Redo step three and four until all remaining VIFs are less than 10.

6. Validate regression model.

Regression ANOVA

Table 8-5 is the ANOVA table design that is used in regression analysis. As part of the overall regression output, the ANOVA table provides us with a summary of the sources of variation within our model.

It should be noted that the r^2 for our regression model can be calculated using information directly from the ANOVA table:

$$r^2 = \frac{SSR}{SST}$$

ANOVA TABLE FOR REGRESSION

Source of Variation	Sum of Squares	Mean Square	F-Value
Regression	$SSR = \Sigma(\hat{Y}_i - \bar{Y}_i)^2$	$MSR = \dfrac{SSR}{d.f.}$	$\dfrac{MSR}{MSE}$
Error	$SSE = \Sigma(Y_i - \hat{Y}_i)^2$	$MSE = \dfrac{SSE}{d.f.}$	
Total	$SST = \Sigma(Y_i - \bar{Y}_i)^2$		

Table 8-5.

In addition to the F-value, a P-value is usually provided as part of regression output. Generally, whenever the ANOVA p-value is less than 0.05, the input variables in the model, as a set, are considered to be useful for predicting the value of the output variable.

Model Validation

The same validation principles that we apply in simple linear regression are applied similarly in multiple regression. In addition, we evaluate our model using:

1. *Variance inflation factor (VIF):* check for the presence of multicollinearity.
2. *Adjusted r^2:* adding input variables to a regression model will always increase r^2. To account for this, an adjusted r^2 is calculated for use in multiple regression.

Example: The general manager of a company that purchases components for the assembly of large air compressors (multiple plant locations), is interested in modeling delivery charges related to the purchased components. Table 8-6 is a partial listing of the shipping data that will be used by the general manager to develop her model.

The general manager believes that delivery charge is a function of four factors: shipment *weight*, shipment *volume*, shipment *distance*, and *number of items shipped*. Using these four factors, she developed the model shown in Table 8-7.

SHIPPING EXAMPLE DATA

Weight (Pounds)	Volume (Feet³)	Distance (Miles)	Items Shipped	Delivery Charge
403	45	71	310	391
377	37	65	250	340
361	36	66	240	353
411	38	62	260	366
—	—	—	—	—
—	—	—	—	—
—	—	—	—	—
652	31	55	210	300
543	43	63	290	342

Table 8-6.

MULTIPLE REGRESSION EXAMPLE

The regression equation is
Delivery Charge = −3.56 + 0.0149 Weight + 5.71 Volume
+ 4.23 Distance − 0.554 Items Shipped

Predictor	Coef	SE Coef	T	P	VIF
Constant	−3.559	9.523	−0.37	0.709	
Weight	0.01486	0.01056	1.41	0.161	1.0
Volume	5.705	2.325	2.45	0.015	155.0
Distance	4.2339	0.2084	20.31	0.000	2.7
Items Shipped	−0.5542	0.3487	−1.59	0.114	156.8

S = 14.5967   R − Sq = 90.3%   R − Sq(adj) = 90.1%

Analysis of Variance

Source	DF	SS	MS	F	P
Regression	4	388614	97153	455.99	0.000
Residual Error	195	41547	213		
Total	199	430161			

Table 8-7.

INTERPRETING THE REGRESSION OUTPUT

1. The regression equation is: Delivery Charge = −3.56 + 0.0149 Weight + 5.71 Volume + 4.23 Distance − 0.554 Items Shipped.

2. Multicollinearity is a problem. *Volume* and *Items Shipped* have very high VIF values (155 and 156.8).

3. The correlation matrix (Table 8-8) shows that *Volume* and *Items Shipped* are strongly correlated at 0.997. The correlation between *Delivery Charge* and *Volume* is 0.834. The correlation between *Delivery Charge* and *Items Shipped* is 0.832. The coefficient of *Items Shipped* is -0.5542, which doesn't make sense (the negative coefficient implies that the number of items shipped reduces the delivery charge).

4. *Items Shipped* should be dropped from the model and the reduced model should be analyzed.

CORRELATION MATRIX

	Weight	Volume	Distance	Items Shipped
Volume	0.093			
Distance	0.112	0.793		
Items Shipped	0.092	0.997	0.795	
Delivery Charge	0.138	0.834	0.938	0.832

Table 8-8.

5. *Items Shipped* is dropped, leaving weight, volume, and distance remaining in the model. The results of the new regression analysis are shown in Table 8-9.

REDUCED REGRESSION MODEL

The regression equation is
Delivery Charge = −5.63 + 0.0151 Weight + 2.04 Volume + 4.20 Distance

Predictor	Coef	SE Coef	T	P	VIF
Constant	−5.627	9.523	−0.37	0.553	
Weight	0.01512	0.01056	1.43	0.155	1.0
Volume	2.0419	0.3076	2.45	0.000	2.7
Distance	4.1979	0.2084	20.31	0.000	2.7

S = 14.6534   R − Sq = 90.2%   R − Sq(adj) = 90.1%

Analysis of Variance

Source	DF	SS	MS	F	P
Regression	3	388075	159358	602.45	0.000
Residual Error	196	42085	215		
Total	199	430161			

Table 8-9.

INTERPRETING THE REGRESSION OUTPUT OF THE REDUCED MODEL (WEIGHT, VOLUME, AND DISTANCE)

1. The regression equation is: Delivery Cost = −5.63 + 0.0151 Weight + 2.04 Volume + 4.20 Distance.
2. *Multicollinearity* is no longer a problem, since all VIF values are less than 10.

3. The model is a very good predictor of delivery charge, since r^2 = 90%.

4. *Weight* is not significant (p = 0.155) and should be dropped from the model and the reduced model be analyzed.

5. *Weight* is dropped, leaving *volume* and *distance* remaining in the model. The results of the new regression analysis are shown in Table 8-10.

REDUCED REGRESSION MODEL

The regression equation is
Delivery Charge = 0.61 + 2.04 Volume + 4.22 Distance

Predictor	Coef	SE Coef	T	P	VIF
Constant	0.606	8.424	0.07	0.943	
Volume	2.0448	0.3084	6.63	0.000	2.7
Distance	4.2167	0.2081	20.26	0.000	2.7

S = 14.6918   R – Sq = 90.1%   R – Sq(adj) = 90.0%

Analysis of Variance

Source	DF	SS	MS	F	P
Regression	2	387638	193819	897.93	0.000
Residual Error	197	42522	216		
Total	199	430161			

Table 8-10.

INTERPRETING THE REGRESSION OUTPUT OF THE REDUCED MODEL (VOLUME AND DISTANCE)

1. The regression equation is: Delivery Charge = 0.61 + 2.04 Volume + 4.22 Distance.
2. Multicollinearity is not a problem, since both VIF values are less than 10.
3. The model is a very good predictor of delivery charge, since the adjusted r^2 = 90%.
4. The p-values for volume and distance are less than 0.05; both are statistically significant and are useful predictors of delivery cost.
5. The regression residuals graphs (Figure 8-8) look good, so the model is appropriate to use.

Multiple Regression Analysis Using Qualitative Input Variables

Qualitative input variables can be used when performing multiple regression. Examples of qualitative variables are: month, shift, region, individual's name, color, etc.

In practice, dummy variables are created to represent the qualitative variables in the regression model, with the total number of dummy variables used in the model equal to the total number of qualitative variables minus one.

In the delivery charge example, the general manager suspects that items requiring special handling add to the total delivery charge, so she adds the qualitative variables special handling and regular handling to the model. An abbreviated matrix of the model's variables is shown in Table 8.11 and the results of the regression analysis are shown in Table 8-12.

REGRESSION RESIDUALS

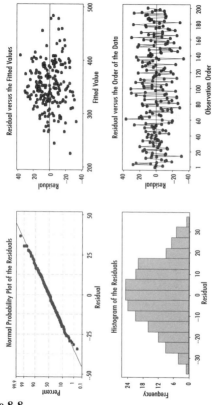

Figure 8-8.

DATA MATRIX WITH INDICATOR VARIABLES

Volume	Distance	Delivery Charge	Special Handling	Regular Handling
45.15	70.5	391.30	1	0
36.50	64.8	340.21	0	1
35.97	66.1	352.58	1	0
38.11	61.6	366.13	1	0
—	—	—	—	—
—	—	—	—	—
—	—	—	—	—
42.05	57.8	325.21	0	1

Table 8-11.

REGRESSION WITH QUALITATIVE VARIABLES

The regression equation is
Delivery Charge = 47.6 + 20.3 Special Handling + 1.03 Volume + 3.44 Distance

Predictor	Coef	SE Coef	T	P	VIF
Constant	47.624	9.640	4.94	0.000	
Special Handling	20.343	2.665	7.63	0.000	2.1
Volume	1.8291	0.2729	6.70	0.000	2.7
Distance	3.4433	0.2093	16.45	0.000	3.5

$$S = 12.9320 \quad R-Sq = 92.4\% \quad R-Sq(adj) = 92.3\%$$

Analysis of Variance

Source	DF	SS	MS	F	P
Regression	3	397383	132461	792.06	0.000
Residual Error	196	32778	167		
Total	199	430161			

Table 8-12.

INTERPRETING REGRESSION OUTPUT WHEN USING QUALITATIVE VARIABLES

The interpretation of regression output when using qualitative variables is essentially the same as when using quantitative variables. The only difference is in the interpretation of the model coefficients. Qualitative variables have a value of either

0 or 1; 1 indicates the presence of some attribute and 0 its absence. Therefore, the coefficient of the qualitative variable is multiplied by 1 when an attribute is present and 0 when absent.

1. The regression equation is: Delivery Charge = 47.6 + 20.30 Special Handling + 1.83 Volume + 3.44 Distance.
2. For *regular handling*, the special handling term drops out and the regression equation becomes: Delivery Charge = 47.6 + 1.83 Volume + 3.44 Distance.
3. For *special handling*, $20.30 is added to the delivery charge (the coefficient for special handling is 20.3).

The use of the qualitative variables in the regression model shows that the delivery charges for special handling are higher than for regular handling.

Example: Estimate the delivery charge for a package having a volume of 45.15 feet^3 and shipped 70.5 miles for both special and regular handling.

1. *Special Handling Delivery Charge:*
   $47.60 + $20.30 (1) + $1.83 (45.15) + $3.44 (70.5)
   = $393.04
2. *Regular Handling Delivery Charge:*
   $47.60 + $20.30 (0) + $1.83 (45.15) + $3.44 (70.5)
   = $372.74

Curvilinear Regression

Curvilinear regression is used to determine the mathematical relationship between input variables and an output variable when the functional relationship is non-linear.

The mathematical model for a second degree regression equation is:

$$\hat{Y}_i = b_0 + b_1 x_i + b_2 x^2_i + e_i$$

where:

$\hat{Y}_i$ is the estimated value of the output variable

b_0 is the y-intercept (value of y when $x = 0$)

b_1 and b_2 are the slopes of the input variables

x_i is the value of the input variable

x^2_i is the squared value of the input variable

e_i is the residual value; a measurement of the difference between the original y-value and the y-value predicted by the regression model.

Example: Figure 8-9 shows a regression line that was fitted to the original data with a linear model. The r^2 for the model is 98.1%, indicating a very good fit. However, upon examination of the model's residual plots (Figure 8-10), a different story unfolds.

The normal probability plot clearly indicates that the residuals are not normal. In addition, the plot of the residuals versus the fitted values is parabolic, suggesting that a quadratic model is appropriate.

Figure 8-11 shows a regression line that was fitted to the original data with a quadratic model. The r^2 for the model is

LINEAR REGRESSION MODEL

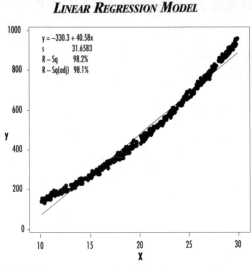

y = −330.3 + 40.58x
s   31.6583
R − Sq   98.2%
R − Sq(adj)   98.1%

Figure 8-9.

99.8%, slightly higher than that of the linear model.

The normal probability plot and the residuals versus the fitted values plot (see Figure 8-12) are normal, indicating that the quadratic model is appropriate to use.

RESIDUAL PLOTS FOR LINEAR MODEL

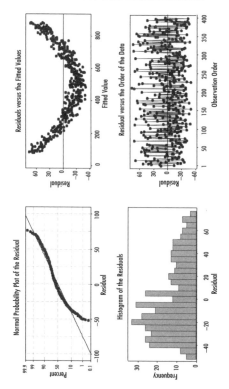

Figure 8-10.

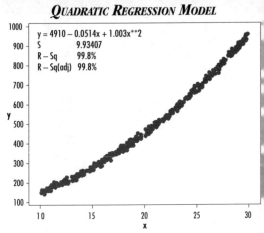

QUADRATIC REGRESSION MODEL

$y = 4910 - 0.0514x + 1.003x^{**}2$
S 9.93407
$R - Sq$ 99.8%
$R - Sq(adj)$ 99.8%

Figure 8-11.

How to Perform Regression Analysis

1. Identify variable relationships using scatter plots, matrix plots, or correlation analysis.

2. Select the appropriate regression model:
   a. Simple linear regression: single, continuous input variable.
   b. Multiple regression: two or more continuous input variables.
   c. Multiple regression with dummy variables: two or more input variables, including at least one qualitative input variable.

RESIDUAL PLOTS FOR QUADRATIC MODEL

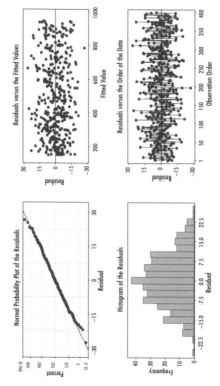

Figure 8-12.

d. Curvilinear regression: single or multiple input variables that have a nonlinear relationship with the output variable.

3. Assess model quality with r^2 (use adjusted r^2 for multiple regression).

4. Assess the significance of the input variables. If an input coefficient's p-value is less than 0.05, the input variable is a useful predictor of the output variable (remove any input variables from the model having a $p > 0.05$).

5. If using multiple regression, test for multicollinearity using variance inflation factors (VIF). If any of the input variables have a VIF > 10, use the *Systematic Procedure for VIF > 10* to make corrections to your model.

6. Perform diagnostic tests to validate your model.
   a. Use a normal probability plot to verify that the residuals are normally distributed.
   b. Use residual plots (residual vs. fitted value, residual vs. time, etc.) to verify constancy of variance of residuals.

7. If diagnostic tests indicate non-normal residuals and/or non-constancy of residuals, investigate using a different model.

CHAPTER NINE
Design of Experiments

What Is Design of Experiments?

Design of Experiments (DOE) is a structured methodology that provides us with a mechanism to observe how the output of a process is affected by specific changes that we make in the settings of the process inputs.

We often use factorial designs (see *Factorial Designs* below) to determine the effect that two or more factors have on our process. All possible combinations of factors and factor levels are involved in the experiment, which allows us to assess both *main effects* and *interaction effects*.

1. *Main Effect:* the effect on the response variable that is produced by changing the settings of an input variable.
2. *Interaction Effect:* the effect on the response variable that is produced by the combination of two or more input variables.

Examples of *process input variables* (factors) are: pressure, temperature, type of material, speed, type of reagent, location, moisture content, etc.

Examples of *process output variables* (responses) are: percent yield, weight, volume, thickness, length, processing cycle-time, etc.

Application of Design of Experiments in Six Sigma

In Six Sigma, design of experiments is used to determine the inputs that have the greatest influence on the output of a process and the settings for those factors that will result in improved process performance.

Factorial Experiments

Six Sigma practitioners have found that often, only two to six factors have a significant effect on process output. Identifying these "vital few" factors and understanding how they affect the process is key to sustained process improvement.

Factorial experiments provide us with an effective approach to test our assumptions concerning process inputs.

DESIGN TERMINOLOGY

1. *Response:* the output variable that is being studied.
2. *Factor:* an input variable that is controllable and is believed to have a measurable effect on the response.
3. *Level:* the magnitude of a quantitative factor (e.g., 25° C versus 50° C) or the attribute of a qualitative factor (e.g., paper versus plastic). Levels are also called settings.
4. *Treatment:* a distinct combination of factors and levels. Treatments are also called runs.
5. *Replicate:* the repetition of an experimental run. Replicates must be independent and should be produced under conditions that are similar to those of the original run.

DESIGN FUNDAMENTALS

The prerequisites for a good experiment require a careful and thoughtful selection of the fundamental elements of the experiment:

1. *Response Selection:* a precise operational definition is a must. In addition, validation of the measurement system will help ensure a successful DOE.

2. *Factor Selection:* it's important to involve people who have good process knowledge when selecting the input factors for the DOE. This should be accomplished using cause and effect analysis.

3. *Level Selection:* we use two levels for each factor in the experiment: low and high. Low is coded as a "−" and high is coded as a "+."

    a. *Quantitative Factors:* here we use two (sometimes three) levels for each factor, which are separate enough in magnitude to cause a measurable change in the response. We will always select factor levels that are within reason, i.e., we never knowingly use a level that will have a destructive effect on the output. For example, if temperature is one of our factors and the process is designed to operate between 15°C and 25°C, we might assign the levels: Low = 15°C and High = 25°C.

    b. *Qualitative Factors:* here we use two (sometimes three) levels for a factor that is associated with an attribute. For example, if we use material supplier as a factor, the two suppliers are arbitrarily assigned a

level, e.g., Low = Howe Corporation and High =
Buchanan Industries.

4. *Treatment:* a specific combination of factors and factor
levels.

Full Factorial Design

Full factorial designs provide us with information regarding
all main effects and interactions. The number of treatments
required in an experiment is defined by:

Number of Factors	Number of Treatments
2	4
3	8
4	16
5	32
6	64
7	128
8	256
9	512
10	1,024

Number of
Factors

2^n

Number of
Levels

Each additional factor added to a full factorial design
doubles the number of treatments. Fractional factorial
designs are usually advised when resources are limited (time,
cost, people).

Figure 9-1 is an example of a design matrix and associated factor settings for a 2^2 full factorial design and Figure 9-2
is an example of a 2^3 full factorial design. In both designs, all

ossible combinations of factors and levels are present. Each
istinct combination (treatment) is run and the value of the
esponse is assigned to that treatment. After all treatments
re run, further analysis is performed to identify which of the
udied factors have a statistically significant effect on the
esponse variable.

EXAMPLE OF A 2^2 FULL FACTORIAL DESIGN

2^2 full factorial	
−	−
+	−
−	+
+	+

Time	Temperature
10	20
15	20
10	30
15	30

Figure 9-1.

EXAMPLE OF A 2^3 FULL FACTORIAL DESIGN

2^3 full factorial		
A	B	C
−	−	−
+	−	−
−	+	−
+	+	−
−	−	+
+	−	+
−	+	+
+	+	+

Time	Temperature	Catalyst
10	20	A
15	20	A
10	30	A
15	30	A
10	20	B
15	20	B
10	30	B
15	30	B

Figure 9-2.

Example: The yield of a chemical manufacturing process is affected by the batch temperature, concentration, and type of catalyst used in the process. An abbreviated version of the full factorial design matrix that was developed to improve process yield is shown in Table 9-1. This is a 2^3 full factorial design with 5 replicates, which means that five duplicate 2^3 experiments are conducted for a total of 40 runs (5 experiments x 8 treatments per experiment). The parameters of the DOE are:

1. Three *factors:* concentration, temperature, and catalyst.
2. Two *levels* for each factor (*low* and *high*):

Factor	Low	High
Concentration	0.10	0.15
Temperature	60°C	75°C
Catalyst	A	B

3. Five *replicates* of each *treatment* (a specific combination of factors and factor levels. Each row in Table 9-1 is a treatment. For example:

Row 1 is the treatment:
   Concentration = 0.10
   Temperature = 60°C
   Catalyst = A

Row 2 is the treatment:
   Concentration = 0.15
   Temperature = 60°C
   Catalyst = A

DESIGN MATRIX (ABBREVIATED)

Concentration	Temperature	Catalyst	Replicate
0.10	60	A	1
0.15	60	A	1
0.10	75	A	1
0.15	75	A	1
0.10	60	B	1
0.15	60	B	1
0.10	75	B	1
0.15	75	B	1
0.10	60	A	2
0.15	60	A	2
0.10	75	A	2
0.15	75	A	2
0.10	60	B	2
0.15	60	B	2
0.10	75	B	2
0.15	75	B	2
—	—	—	—
—	—	—	—
—	—	—	—
0.15	75	B	5

Table 9-1.

How Do I Know Which Process Factors Are Significant?

We can determine which factors have statistically significant effects on the response by looking at the output in Table 9-2.

The main effects and interactions with a p-value of less than 0.05 have a statistically significant effect on the response. The significant factors in the example, i.e., those factors that have an effect on process yield are: *concentration* ($p=0.000$), *temperature* ($p = 0.000$), and the interaction of *concentration* and *catalyst* ($p = 0.029$).

FACTORIAL EXPERIMENT OUTPUT

Factorial Fit: Yield versus Concentration, Temperature, Catalyst					
Estimated Effects and Coefficients for Yield in Coded Units					
Term	Effect	Coef	SE Coef	T	P
Constant		0.096733	0.001413	684.76	0.000
Concentration	**−0.02222**	**−0.01111**	**0.001413**	**−7.86**	**0.000**
Temperature	**0.01522**	**0.00761**	**0.001413**	**5.39**	**0.000**
Catalyst	0.00059	0.00030	0.001413	0.21	0.834
Concentration x Temperature	−0.00203	−0.00102	0.001413	−0.72	0.475
Concentration x Catalyst	**0.00634**	**0.00317**	**0.001413**	**2.25**	**0.029**
Temperature x Catalyst	0.00553	0.00277	0.001413	1.96	0.075
Concentration x Temperature x Catalyst	−0.00184	−0.000092	0.001413	−0.65	0.517
$S = 0.0113012$ $R-Sq = 64.27\%$ $R-Sq(adj) = 59.80\%$					

Table 9-2.

PARETO CHART OF STANDARDIZED EFFECTS

We can also use a standardized effects Pareto chart to identify significant effects (Figure 9-3). A significant effect is indicated en a bar extends beyond the significance limit. The significance limit is the t-value corresponding to $t_{(\alpha, d.f.)}$. We normally use an α equal to 0.05; to determine $d.f.$, we use the formula:

$$d.f. = (\text{\# of observations} - 1)(\text{\# of runs})$$

In our example (Table 9-2), we have eight observations in ch run (each run is a replicate), so:

$$d.f. = (8 - 1) \times 8 = 56$$

We can use Excel to determine the value for

$t_{(0.05, 56)}$, as follows:

$$\text{TINV } (0.05, 56) = 2.003$$

Note in Table 9.2 that each of the significant factors has a value (ignore the negative signs) greater than 2.003.

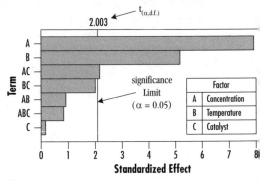

PARETO CHART OF STANDARDIZED EFFECTS

Factor	
A	Concentration
B	Temperature
C	Catalyst

Figure 9-3.

How Can We Determine the Value of the Significant Effects?

The magnitude of the significant effects can be determined using *main effects* and *interaction plots* (refer to Chapter 10 for more information on these plots).

1. *Main Effects Plot:* displays the effect that a specific factor has on the average value of the response. Figure 9-4 shows the main effects plots for concentration and temperature.

   Interpreting the Plots: a concentration of 0.10 produce an average yield of about 98% versus a concentration o 0.15, which produces an average yield of about 95.5%. Also, a temperature of 75°C versus 60°C will cause the average yield to increase about 1.5% (from 96% to 97.5%).

2. *Interaction Plot:* displays the effect that the combination of factors has on the average value of the response. Figure 9-5 shows the interaction plot for concentration and catalyst.

   Interpreting the Plot: when concentration is at 15%, going from catalyst A to catalyst B increases the average yield. Similarly, when the concentration is at 10%, going from catalyst A to catalyst B decreases the average yield. The highest yield occurs when catalyst A is used with a concentration of 10%.

Predicting Process Output Using the Results of Our Factorial Experiment

We can now define a model for predicting process output, using our results from the factorial experiment. To begin, we remove the terms from the factorial design that aren't significant and repeat the analysis. Table 9-3 shows the output from the chemical manufacturing example, using a reduced model with the insignificant terms removed (note: factors showing insignificant main effects that produce significant interaction effects are kept in the model).

MAIN EFFECTS PLOTS

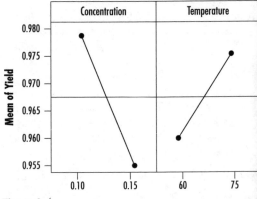

Figure 9-4.

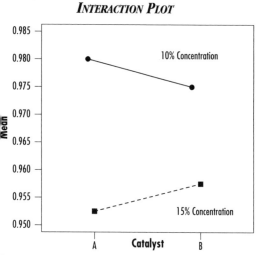

INTERACTION PLOT

- 10% Concentration
- 15% Concentration

Mean (y-axis: 0.950 to 0.985)

Catalyst (x-axis: A, B)

Figure 9-5.

The output from our analysis of the results from the factorial experiment shows that the factors in our model explain 98.59% of the variation in process yield (see R – Sq (adj) in Table 9-3).

We define our model using the coefficients in the DOE output. If your DOE software uses both coded and uncoded values for model coefficients, be sure to use the coefficients that are uncoded for the final prediction equation (see example below). Also, when qualitative factors are included in the model, use –1 for low level and 1 for high level in the prediction equation.

Using the output from our example in Table 9-3, we state the equation to predict process output:

Yield = 0.954 − 0.444 concentration + 0.001 temperature − 0.015 catalyst + 0.127 concentration x catalyst

Example: Predict process yield, given the following factors and levels:

1. Concentration = 0.10
2. Temperature = 75°C
3. Catalyst = A = −1

Yield = 0.954 − (0.444)(0.10) + (0.001)(75) − (0.015)(−1) + (0.127)(0.10)(−1) = 98.7%

Table 9-4 shows the predicted results for all factor combinations. The greatest predicted yield (98.7%) is achieved with the following settings: concentration = 0.10, temperature = 75°C, and catalyst = A.

REDUCED MODEL (DOE)

Factorial Fit: Yield versus Concentration, Temperature, Catalyst

Estimated Effects and Coefficients for Yield (Coded Units)

Term	Effect	Coef	SE Coef	T	P
Constant		0.096733	0.001434	674.69	0.000
Concentration	−0.02222	−0.01111	0.001434	−7.75	0.000
Temperature	0.01522	0.00761	0.001434	5.31	0.000
Catalyst	0.00059	0.00030	0.001434	0.21	0.837
Concentration x Catalyst	0.00634	0.00317	0.001434	2.21	0.031

$S = 0.0114700$ $R - Sq = 61.22\%$ $R - Sq(adj) = 58.59\%$

Estimated Coefficients for Yield Using Data in Uncoded Units

Term	Coef	
Constant	0.954	
Concentration	−0.444	Model
Temperature	0.001	Coefficients
Catalyst	−0.015	
Concentration x Catalyst	0.127	

Table 9-3.

YIELD PREDICTIONS

Concentration	Temperature	Catalyst (A=−1, B=1)	Yield
0.10	75	−1	98.7%
0.10	75	1	98.2%
0.15	75	−1	95.8%
0.15	75	1	96.6%
0.10	60	−1	97.2%
0.10	60	1	96.7%
0.15	60	−1	94.3%
0.15	60	1	95.1%

Table 9-4.

Randomization and Blocking

RANDOMIZATION

All processes are subject to the effects of unknown or uncontrollable factors that systematically affect their output. An example is a pressure regulator for an air supply line that doesn't provide a constant air pressure and is unknown to management. Randomization of runs is used to help guard against systematic effects that could affect the results of your DOE. In practice, this involves the random selection and running of the treatments. DOE software automatically provides randomized design matrices.

Figure 9-6 is a comparison of a standard design and a randomized version of the same design. Note that the treatments in the randomized design are ordered differently than hose in the standard design. For example, row 1 in the standard matrix is row 6 in the randomized matrix.

STANDARD AND RANDOMIZED DESIGNS

Standard Design			Randomized Design		
A	B	C	A	B	C
−	−	−	+	−	+
+	−	−	+	−	−
−	+	−	−	+	−
+	+	−	+	+	+
−	−	+	−	+	+
+	−	+	−	−	−
−	+	+	−	−	+
+	+	+	+	+	−

Figure 9-6.

RANDOMIZED BLOCK DESIGN (BLOCKING)

Randomized treatments should be run under similar conditions (e.g., during one shift, using material from the same producer, etc.). When this isn't possible, we use a *randomized block design*.

Example: consider a plastic molding company that purchases material from two different suppliers and it is known that slight differences in the material properties have an effect on the process output. If we run an experiment using material from the different suppliers, we need to create separate experimental blocks that are defined by the material supplier.

Table 9-5 is the *randomized block design* that was developed for the molding company. Note that each supplier is assigned to a block and the treatments are randomized within each block. The treatments were then run separately for each block and the defect rates were recorded for each treatment. The results of the DOE are shown in Table 9-6 and Figures 9-7 and 9-8.

RANDOMIZED BLOCK DESIGN

Block	Supplier	Temperature	PSI	Extruder
	JH	50	200	B
	JH	50	225	B
	JH	40	225	A
1	JH	40	200	A
	JH	40	225	B
	JH	50	225	A
	JH	50	200	A
	JH	40	200	B
	WL	40	225	A
	WL	50	225	A
	WL	50	200	A
2	WL	50	225	B
	WL	40	200	B
	WL	40	225	B
	WL	40	200	A
	WL	50	200	B

Table 9-5.

In Table 9-6, we find that temperature ($p=0.000$) and PS ($p=0.007$) have an effect on defect rate. We also note that here is no *Block* effect (p = 0.300). Recall that we blocked on the supplier and the high p-value indicates that the material supplier doesn't affect the defect rate. No interaction effects are indicated and the main effects plots (Figure 9-8) how that the defect level is smallest when temperature is low 40) and PSI is high (225).

RESULTS OF RANDOMIZED BLOCK DOE

Factorial Fit: Defect Rate versus Block Temperature, PSI, Extruder					
Estimated Effects and Coefficients for Defect Rate (Coded Units)					
Term	Effect	Coef	SE Coef	T	P
Constant		0.054183	0.002402	22.56	0.000
Block		0.002355	0.002236	1.05	0.300
Temperature	0.019911	0.009956	0.002411	4.13	0.000
PSI	−0.013913	−0.006956	0.002406	−2.89	0.007
Extruder	0.007778	0.003889	0.002401	1.62	.0115
Temperature x PSI	0.003661	0.001831	0.002411	0.76	0.454
Temperature x Extruder	0.007852	0.003926	0.002401	1.64	0.112
PSI x Extruder	0.002557	0.001279	0.002415	0.53	0.600
Temperature x PSI x Extruder	0.001602	0.000801	0.002401	0.33	0.741

Table 9-6.

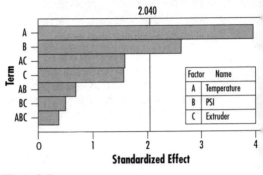

PARETO FOR RANDOMIZED BLOCK DOE

Factor	Name
A	Temperature
B	PSI
C	Extruder

Figure 9-7.

Fractional Factorial Designs

Fractional factorial designs are utilized whenever it is desired to reduce the number of experimental runs. We often use these designs to screen for the key factors in a process. Screening DOEs usually involve starting with a large number of potential key factors and using a fractional factorial experiment to narrow them down to a much smaller group of factors. Then, another DOE is conducted using the results of the screening DOE.

As the name implies, a fractional factorial design requires only a fraction of the number of runs that would be required with a full factorial design, using the same number of factors. The economy resulting from using a fractional factorial design is clear when you consider that a 10 factor

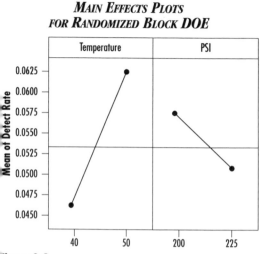

MAIN EFFECTS PLOTS
FOR RANDOMIZED BLOCK DOE

Figure 9-8.

full factorial experiment (without replication) requires 1,024 runs and a 1/8 fractional factorial design requires only 128 runs. The trade-off in using fractional factorial versus full factorial designs is a confounding of the main effects and the interaction effects.

Confounding and Design Resolution

When we remove runs from a design (as we do with fractional factorial designs), we lose some of our ability to distinguish which of the factors have a measurable effect on the response. This inability to distinguish factors is called confounding. The degree of confounding is dependent on the fraction selected for the design.

Design Resolution

The resolution of a design indicates the pattern of confounding in our design. The three most important of the design resolutions are:

1. *Resolution III Designs:*
   a. None of the main effects are confounded with other main effects.
   b. Main effects are confounded with two-factor interactions.

2. *Resolution IV Designs:*
   a. None of the main effects are confounded with other main effects or two-factor interactions.
   b. Two-factor interactions are confounded with other two-factor interactions.

3. *Resolution V Designs:*
   a. None of the main effects are confounded with other main effects or two-factor interactions.
   b. Two-factor interactions are confounded with three-factor interactions.

Design Notation

Fractional factorial designs are identified by a shorthand notation that includes the number of levels, design fraction, and design resolution. The example below is a ½ fraction, resolution III design. The fraction is determined as follows:

1. $2^4 = 16$
2. $2^{4-1} = 2^3 = 8$
3. 8 is ½ of 16

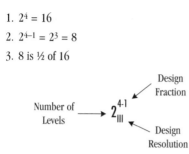

DESIGN MATRICES

Tables 9-7 through 9-13 are a few common fractional factorial design matrices for use with three to six factors with varying resolutions of III to VI.

2^{3-1} FRACTIONAL FACTORIAL DESIGN

2_{III}^{3-1} 1/2 Fraction Resolution III		
A	B	C
−	−	+
+	−	−
−	+	−
+	+	+

Table 9-7.

2^{4-1} Fractional Factorial Design

2_{IV}^{4-1} 1/2 Fraction Resolution IV			
A	B	C	D
−	−	−	−
+	−	−	+
−	+	−	+
+	+	−	−
−	−	+	+
+	−	+	−
−	+	+	−
+	+	+	+

Table 9-8.

2^{5-1} Fractional Factorial Design

2_{V}^{5-1} 1/2 Fraction Resolution V				
A	B	C	D	E
−	−	−	−	+
+	−	−	−	−
−	+	−	−	−
+	+	−	−	+
−	−	+	−	−
+	−	+	−	+
−	+	+	−	+
+	+	+	−	−

Table 9-9. (Continued on next page)

2^{5-1} FRACTIONAL FACTORIAL DESIGN

2_V^{5-1} 1/2 Fraction Resolution V				
A	B	C	D	E
−	−	−	+	−
+	−	−	+	+
−	+	−	+	+
+	+	−	+	−
−	−	+	+	+
+	−	+	+	−
−	+	+	+	−
+	+	+	+	+

Table 9-9. (Continued)

2^{5-2} FRACTIONAL FACTORIAL DESIGN

2_{III}^{5-2} 1/4 Fraction Resolution III				
A	B	C	D	E
−	−	−	+	+
+	−	−	−	−
−	+	−	−	+
+	+	−	+	−
−	−	+	+	−
+	−	+	−	+
−	+	+	−	−
+	+	+	+	+

Table 9-10.

2_{VI}^{6-1} 1/2 Fraction Resolution VI					
A	B	C	D	E	F
−	−	−	−	−	−
+	−	−	−	−	+
−	+	−	−	−	+
+	+	−	−	−	−
−	−	+	−	−	+
+	−	+	−	−	−
−	+	+	−	−	−
+	+	+	−	−	+
−	−	−	+	−	+
+	−	−	+	−	−
−	+	−	+	−	−
+	+	−	+	−	+
−	−	+	+	−	−
+	−	+	+	−	+
−	+	+	+	−	+
+	+	+	+	−	−
−	−	−	−	+	+
+	−	−	−	+	−
−	+	−	−	+	−
+	+	−	−	+	+
−	−	+	−	+	−
+	−	+	−	+	+
−	+	+	−	+	+
+	+	+	−	+	−

Table 9-11. (Continued on next page)

2^{6-1} FRACTIONAL FACTORIAL DESIGN

2_{VI}^{6-1} 1/2 Fraction Resolution VI					
A	B	C	D	E	F
−	−	−	+	+	−
+	−	−	+	+	+
−	+	−	+	+	+
+	+	−	+	+	−
−	−	+	+	+	+
+	−	+	+	+	−
−	+	+	+	+	−
+	+	+	+	+	+

Table 9-11. (Continued)

2^{6-2} FRACTIONAL FACTORIAL DESIGN

2_{IV}^{6-2} 1/4 Fraction Resolution IV					
A	B	C	D	E	F
−	−	−	−	−	−
+	−	−	−	+	−
−	+	−	−	+	+
+	+	−	−	−	+
−	−	+	−	+	+
+	−	+	−	−	+
−	+	+	−	−	−
+	+	+	−	+	−

Table 9-12. (Continued on next page)

2^{6-2} Fractional Factorial Design

2_{IV}^{6-2} 1/4 Fraction Resolution IV					
A	B	C	D	E	F
−	−	−	+	−	+
+	−	−	+	+	+
−	+	−	+	+	−
+	+	−	+	−	−
−	−	+	+	+	−
+	−	+	+	−	−
−	+	+	+	−	+
+	+	+	+	+	+

Table 9-12. (Continued)

2^{6-3} Fractional Factorial Design

2_{III}^{6-3} 1/8 Fraction Resolution III					
A	B	C	D	E	F
−	−	−	+	+	+
+	−	−	−	−	+
−	+	−	−	+	−
+	+	−	+	−	−
−	−	+	+	−	−
+	−	+	−	+	−
−	+	+	−	−	+
+	+	+	+	+	+

Table 9-13.

Example: an electroplating business is required to meet a plating thickness specification of between 120 mils and 150 mils. By keeping the thickness on the lower end of the specification, the company will achieve significant cost savings. The process factors identified as being potentially significant in controlling plating thickness are: plating tank used, material supplier, solution flow rate and electrical current. A process engineer has the approval to conduct 16 runs. Because he desires to replicate the experiment, he chooses a fractional factorial design. Table 9-14 is the randomized design matrix that was used and Table 9-15 gives the results of the DOE.

PLATING DESIGN MATRIX

Replicate	Tank	Material	Flow Rate	Current	Thickness
	12	CJ8	4	12.5	0.130
	12	CJ8	4	12.5	0.140
	12	CJ8	2	14.5	0.179
1	19	CB4	2	14.5	0.172
	19	CJ8	4	14.5	0.169
	19	CB4	4	12.5	0.145
	19	CJ8	2	12.5	0.170
	19	CB4	4	12.5	0.140
	19	CB4	2	14.5	0.163
	12	CJ8	2	14.5	0.172
	19	CJ8	2	12.5	0.153
2	19	CJ8	4	14.5	0.169
	12	CB4	4	14.5	0.130
	12	CB4	2	12.5	0.155
	12	CB4	4	14.5	0.155
	12	CB4	2	12.5	0.130

Table 9-14.

RESULTS OF 2_{IV}^{4-1} EXPERIMENT

Factorial Fit: Thickness versus Tank, Material, Flow Rate, Current					
Estimated Effects and Coefficients for Thickness (Coded Units)					
Term	Effect	Coef	SE Coef	T	P
Constant		0.154500	0.002647	58.36	0.000
Tank	0.011250	0.005625	0.002647	2.12	0.066
Material	0.011500	0.005750	0.002647	2.17	0.062
Flow Rate	−0.014500	−0.007250	0.002647	−2.74	0.025
Current	0.018250	0.009125	0.002647	3.45	0.009
Tank x Material	−0.001250	−0.000625	0.002647	−0.24	0.819
Tank x Flow Rate	0.005750	0.002875	0.002647	1.09	0.309
Tank x Current	−0.002000	−0.001000	0.002647	−0.38	0.715

Table 9-15.

The factors that have an effect on thickness are flow rate ($p=0.025$) and current ($p=0.009$); there are no interaction effects. Since this is a resolution IV design, none of the main effects are confounded with other main effects.

Recall that in a resolution IV design, two-factor interactions are confounded, meaning that the effects of *Tank*Material*, *Tank*Flow Rate*, and *Tank*Current* are indistinguishable. However, Table 9-15 shows that all two-factor interactions in the model are statistically insignificant (p-values greater than 0.05), so further analysis of the two-factor interactions is unnecessary (also see Figure 9-9).

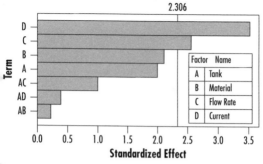

Figure 9-9.

The main effects plots for flow rate and current (Figure 9-10) indicate that a high level for flow rate and a low level for current will produce a lower average thickness.

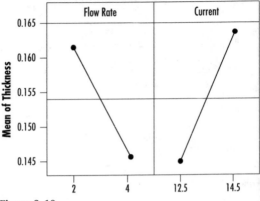

MAIN EFFECTS PLOT FOR PLATING PROCESS

Figure 9-10.

How to Perform a DOE

1. Clearly define the problem or improvement that you wish to address.

2. Define the response (output) variable and provide it with a clear operational definition.

3. Select the input factors that will be included in the DOE.

4. Determine the appropriate design to use:
   a. Full factorial design
   b. Randomized block design
   c. Fractional factorial design

5. Randomize the experimental runs.

6. Conduct the experiment and analyze data.

7. Make recommendations for further study; provide an action plan to improve the process.

CHAPTER TEN
Analysis of Variance (ANOVA)

What Is Analysis of Variance?

A nalysis of variance, commonly referred to as ANOVA, is a general-purpose tool that allows us to:

1. Perform hypothesis testing on more than two population means. For example, we may be interested in comparing the performance of several processes, machines, or people. ANOVA provides a convenient way to do this without having us resort to running multiple t-tests.

2. Understand complex relationships between variables (e.g., variables that are related only over a part of a range of observed values, i.e., interactions among variables) or to evaluate the effects that qualitative variables have on a response (e.g., the brand of toothpaste used versus the number of dental cavities observed).

Application of ANOVA in Six Sigma

In Six Sigma, ANOVA is used to perform Gage R and R (repeatability & reproducibility), to quantify differences in the performance of multiple factors (machines, customers, product types, etc.), to determine the effect that multiple input variables have on process performance (output), and to validate process improvement actions.

One-Way ANOVA

One-way ANOVA is used to compare the means of multiple

populations or processes using a single comparison factor, such as geographic location or color product packaging.

The mathematical model for one-way ANOVA is:

$$X_{ij} = \mu + r_i + \varepsilon_{j(i)}$$

where:

X_{ij} is the observed data

μ is the population mean

r_i is the effect of the factor (row effect)

$\varepsilon_{j(i)}$ is the effect of random error

The general form of the ANOVA hypothesis test is:

H_o: $\mu_1 = \mu_2 = \mu_3 = \ldots = \mu_n$

H_a: At least one of the means is different

Example: The daily performance of five packing machine operators is shown in Table 10-1. A random sample of 25 observations was taken of the daily number of orders packaged by each of the operators. Is there a difference in the average performance of the operators (use $\alpha = 0.05$)?

MACHINE OPERATOR PERFORMANCE

Operator	1	2	3	4	—	—	25
1	39	66	74	52	—	—	67
2	65	52	38	67	—	—	55
3	62	61	60	56	—	—	54
4	55	85	74	75	—	—	63
5	49	49	53	50	—	—	45

Observations (spanning columns 1–25)

Table 10-1.

The hypothesis test is stated as:

H_0: $\mu_{OP1} = \mu_{OP2} = \mu_{OP3} = \mu_{OP4} = \mu_{OP5}$

H_a: At least one of the operators is different

Looking at Table 10-2, we see that p=0.000. Since $p < \alpha$, we reject H_0; at least one of the five operators is different from the others.

ONE-WAY ANOVA RESULTS

One-Way ANOVA: Op1, Op2, Op3, Op4, Op5					
Analysis of Variance					
Source	DF	SS	MS	F	P
Factor	4	4301	1075	10.17	0.000
Error	120	12688	106		
Total	124	16989			

Table 10-2.

HOW TO READ A ONE-WAY ANOVA TABLE

The one-way ANOVA table consists of five columns (p is added in Minitab):

1. *Source:* the components of variation, listed in the following order:
   a. *Factor* is the variable being evaluated (e.g., factor in Table 10-2 is the variable operator).
   b. *Error* represents the random factors that contribute to the total variation.
   c. *Total* is the combination of the variation due to factor and error.

2. *DF:* degrees of freedom, where r is the number of factors and c is the number of observations for each factor, e.g., the number of operators is 5 and the number of observations for each operator is 25. DF is calculated as follows:
   a. *Factor* = $r - 1$
   b. *Error* = $r(c - 1)$
   c. *Total* = $n - 1$
3. *SS:* sum of squares variance estimate
4. *MS:* mean square estimate; equal to SS ÷ DF
5. *F:* equal to $MS_{Factor} \div MS_{Error}$

Two-Way ANOVA

Two-way ANOVA is used to compare the means of multiple populations or processes, using two factors, such as geographic location and machine type or package color and material.

The mathematical model for two-way ANOVA is:

$$X_{ij} = \mu + r_i + c_j + \varepsilon_{ji}$$

where:

X_{ij} is the observed data

μ is the population mean

r_i is the effect of factor 1 (row effect)

c_j is the effect of factor 2 (column effect)

ε_{ji} is the effect of random error

Example: The sourcing department of a large machine tool manufacturer is evaluating the feasibility of purchasing new gages from a lower priced supplier. The new supplier claims that their gages will give the same results as the older, more expensive gages. An evaluation was conducted, using four different operators, each measuring the same standard part twice for each gage (Table 10-3). Is there a difference between the new and old gages (use $\alpha = 0.05$)?

OPERATOR AND GAGE PERFORMANCE DATA

	Operator 1		Operator 2		Operator 3		Operator 4	
Gage	1	2	1	2	1	2	1	2
OLD	0.49	0.51	0.48	0.51	0.61	0.59	0.75	0.74
NEW	0.66	0.74	0.65	0.67	0.56	0.67	0.85	0.75

Table 10-3.

The hypothesis test is stated as:

H_0: $\mu_1 = \mu_2 = \mu_3 = \mu_4 = \mu_5$

H_a: At least one of the means is different

Referring to Table 10-4, the result for operator is $p = 0.087$ and for gage is $p = 0.001$. This indicates that there is a difference between the new and old gages at a 0.05 significance level. Also, it should be noted that there isn't evidence of a difference in the measurement results due to the operator.

TWO-WAY ANOVA WITH REPLICATION—INTERACTION EFFECTS

Two-way ANOVA with replication is used when it is believed that an interaction effect is present. An example of a common interaction is the effect that two or more prescription drugs have on a patient when administered simultaneously.

The mathematical model for two-way ANOVA with replication is:

$$X_{ij} = \mu + r_i + c_j + rc_{ij} + \varepsilon_{k(ij)}$$

TWO-WAY ANOVA RESULTS

Two-Way ANOVA: Measurement versus Gage, Operator					
Analysis of Variance for Measurement					
Source	DF	SS	MS	F	P
Gage	1	0.08556	0.08556	21.75	0.001
Operator	3	0.03347	0.01116	2.84	0.087
Error	11	0.04327	0.00393		
Total	15	0.16229			

Table 10-4.

where:

x_{ij} is the observed data

μ is the population mean

τ_i is the effect of factor 1 (row effect)

β_j is the effect of factor 2 (column effect)

$\tau\beta_{ij}$ is the effect of the interaction of factor 1 and factor 2

$\epsilon_{k(ij)}$ is the effect of random error

Example: A circuit board etching process requires the use of a catalyst in an acid bath. A test is performed using 5 replicates with two different types of catalysts (A & B) and two different acidity levels (10% and 15%). The test results are shown in Table 10-5. Is there a difference in catalysts and acidity levels? Is there a significant interaction effect? Use a significance level $\alpha = 0.05$.

The results, as shown in Table 10-6, are:

a. Acidity: p = 0.070

b. Catalyst: p = 0.001
c. Interaction: p = 0.049

This indicates that at a 0.05 significance level, yield is affected by type of catalyst used (A vs. B). There also appears to be a statistically significant effect due to the interaction between acidity and catalyst.

TEST RESULTS (YIELD)

Acidity Level	Catalyst	
	A	B
10%	0.75	0.81
	0.75	0.78
	0.63	0.79
	0.75	0.83
	0.82	0.84
15%	0.43	0.86
	0.74	0.79
	0.70	0.78
	0.63	0.84
	0.50	0.81

Table 10-5.

TWO-WAY ANOVA (REPLICATED)

Two-Way ANOVA: Yield versus Acidity, Catalyst

Analysis of Variance for Yield

Source	DF	SS	MS	F	P
Acidity	1	0.02245	0.02245	3.77	0.070
Catalyst	1	0.10225	0.10225	17.16	0.001
Interaction	1	0.02665	0.02665	4.47	0.049
Error	16	0.09532	0.00596		
Total	19	0.24666			

Table 10-6.

HOW TO READ A TWO-WAY ANOVA TABLE

The two-way ANOVA table is similar to the one-way table. The difference is the addition of the column factor and also interaction factor when replicates are employed.

1. *Source:* the components of variation, listed in the following order:
   a. *Row Factor* (e.g., acidity in Table 10-6)
   b. *Column Factor* (e.g., catalyst in Table 10-6)
   c. *Interaction Factor* (e.g., interaction in Table 10-6)
   d. *Error* (random variability)
   e. *Total* (combination of the row, column, interaction, and error variances)
2. *DF:* degrees of freedom, calculated as follows:
   a. *Total* = $(n - 1)$
   b. *Row:* $r - 1$
   c. *Column:* $c - 1$

d. *Interaction:* $(r - 1)(c - 1)$
e. *Error* = Total DF − (Row DF + Column DF + Interaction DF)

3. *SS:* sum of squares variance estimate
4. *MS:* mean square estimate; equal to SS ÷ DF
5. *F:* calculated for each of the non-random factors:
   a. *Row* = $MS_{Row} \div MS_{Error}$
   b. *Column* = $MS_{Column} \div MS_{Error}$
   c. *Interaction* = $MS_{Interaction} \div MS_{Error}$

Nested ANOVA

Nested ANOVA is used to perform hierarchical analysis of variance. The ANOVA techniques discussed previously were *crossed*, i.e., every factor under evaluation is combined with each of the other factors (e.g., in the gage example of Table 10-4, every gage is combined with every operator (see Figure 10-1).

In nested designs, we designate main factors and corresponding subgroup factors. Subgroup factors that are nested within one hierarchy cannot be compared to other factors outside of their hierarchy. Figure 10-2 is a nested design for a plastic parts molding process.

The *main factor* is the mold *cavity*, the *subgroup factor* is *sample* $(S_1$ and $S_2)$, and the measurement is part *weight* $(W_1, W_2,$ and $W_3)$. The main factors are not linked to one another (as with a crossed design) and each of the main factors flows down to lower-level subgroups, forming a hierarchy.

CROSSED ANOVA EXAMPLE

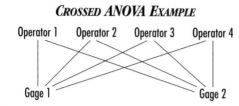

Figure 10-1.

NESTED ANOVA DESIGN

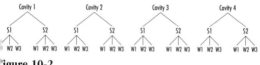

Figure 10-2.

The mathematical model for the nested design in Figure 10-2 is:

$$X_{ijk} = \mu + C_i + S_{j(i)} + \varepsilon_{k(ij)}$$

where:

X_{ijk} is the observed data (part weight)

μ is the population mean

C_i is main factor (cavity)

$S_{j(i)}$ is the subgroup factor (sample)

$\varepsilon_{k(ij)}$ is the effect of random error

Example: A four-cavity mold is used to produce plastic bases for automotive fog lamps. Is there a difference in the weight (Table 10-7) of the parts within each of the mold's cavities? Is there a difference between cavities? Use $\alpha = 0.05$.

PART WEIGHT MEASUREMENTS

	Cavity 1		Cavity 2		Cavity 3		Cavity 4	
Sample	1	2	1	2	1	2	1	2
W1	13.5	12.5	15.0	13.0	12.0	12.0	11.1	12.5
W2	14.0	13.0	14.0	13.5	12.6	11.5	10.5	11.0
W3	13.8	12.8	13.0	13.6	11.0	12.1	12.0	13.0

Table 10-7.

Table 10-8 shows that there is no evidence of a difference in the weights of the parts within each of the cavities, since p = 0.155 (sample). However, p = 0.047 (cavity) indicates that there is a difference between cavities at the 0.05 significance level.

VARIANCE COMPONENTS

In nested ANOVA, the total variation includes the variation of all the nested factors. We can determine the relative effect that each factor has on total variation by identifying the components of variation. To illustrate, refer to the Variance Components output at the bottom of Table 10-8. The molding process variance for part weight is estimated to be 1.447 (total variance). The total variance is broken down into its components:

    a. *Cavity* = 0.852 (58.87%)
    b. *Sample* = 0.140 (9.69 %)
    c. *Error* = 0.455 (31.44%)

So, 58.87% of the total variation is due to differences in the mold cavities. The variation within each cavity contribute

nly 9.69% to the total variance. The remaining 31.44% may
e attributed to random variation or some other factor or
actors that have yet to be identified.

NESTED ANOVA RESULTS

Nested ANOVA: Weight versus Cavity, Sample					

Analysis of Variance for Weight

Source	DF	SS	MS	F	P
Cavity	3	17.9617	5.9872	6.836	0.047
Sample	4	3.5033	0.8758	1.925	0.155
Error	16	7.2800	0.4550		
Total	23	28.7450			

Variance Components

Source	Var Comp.	% of Total	StDev
Cavity	0.852	58.87	0.923
Sample	0.140	9.69	0.375
Error	0.455	31.44	0.675
Total	1.447		1.203

able 10-8.

nalysis of Means

nalysis of Means, commonly referred to as ANOM, is used to
est for differences between factor means and the overall
ean, similarly to one and two-way ANOVA.

The ANOM chart is a plot of the means for each of the
ndividual factors, relative to the mean of all factors com-

bined (grand mean). In addition, upper and lower decision limits are calculated and placed above and below the grand mean. A factor is considered to be significant, only if its mean falls outside of either decision limit.

Example: Apply ANOM to evaluate the performance of the packing operators from Tables 10-1 and 10-2. Use $\alpha = 0.05$.

In Figure 10-3, we see that the average level of performance for operator 4 (Op4) is greater than that for all of the other operators, since the average for Op4 falls outside of the upper decision limit at a 0.05 significance level. Because all of the remaining operators' averages lie within the upper and lower

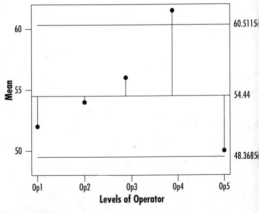

Figure 10-3.

decision limits, they may be performing at the same average level and their differences could be due to random variation.

Main Effects Plots

Main effects plots are used to determine the impact that differing levels of an input variable have on the average level of the response variable. When we evaluate the impact that one factor has on a given response, the result is called a *main effect*. Figure 10-4 is an example of a main effects plot, generated using the data from Table 10-5 (circuit board etching process).

The y-axis of the main effects plot is the response variable (yield) and the x-axis is the input variable (catalyst). A look at Figure 10-4 shows that when catalyst A is used, the average yield is less than 70%. However, when catalyst B is used, the average yield increases to more than 80%. So, it appears that we should use catalyst B to maximize our yield. Before we make a final decision, we should test the significance of the catalyst's effect.

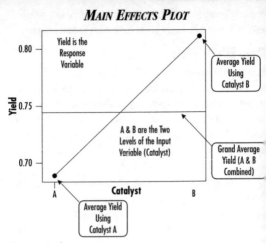

MAIN EFFECTS PLOT

Yield is the Response Variable

Average Yield Using Catalyst B

A & B are the Two Levels of the Input Variable (Catalyst)

Grand Average Yield (A & B Combined)

Catalyst

Average Yield Using Catalyst A

Figure 10-4.

The ANOVA output from Table 10-6 shows that for catalyst, p=0.001, meaning that catalyst is significant at the 0.05 level. Therefore, catalyst B should be used.

Example: We saw that the type of catalyst used in the circuit board etching process had a significant effect on yield. Evaluate the acidity level for main effect, using a significance level of 0.05 (refer to Table 10-6 for ANOVA output).

Looking at Figure 10-5, it appears that yield decreases when the acidity level is higher (15%). However, the ANOVA output from Table 10-6 shows that for acidity, p=0.070, meaning that acidity is not statistically significant at the 0.05

evel, i.e, there isn't enough evidence to suggest that there is
a difference in yield between the 10% and 15% acidity levels.

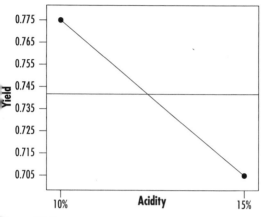

ACIDITY MAIN EFFECTS PLOT

Figure 10-5.

Interaction Plots

Interaction plots are used to determine if there are effects on
the response variable that are produced by the combination
of two or more input variables. Figure 10-6 is an interaction
plot generated using the data from the circuit board etching
process (Table 10-5). Interactions are indicated whenever
the two lines are not parallel. The highest degree of interaction occurs when the two lines form a cross.

INTERACTION PLOT

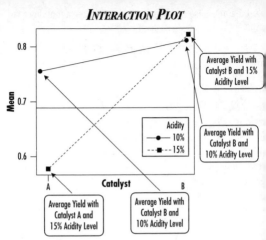

Figure 10-6.

Example: Referring to Figure 10-6 and Table 10-6, determine if an interaction effect is present and identify the levels for both catalyst and acidity that result in the greatest yield (use a 0.05 significance level).

It appears that there is a statistically significant interaction effect with catalyst and acidity because:

a. The 10% and 15% acidity lines cross, suggesting a very strong interaction effect (Figure 10-6).

b. The interaction effect is statistically significant, having a p-value equal to 0.049 (Table 10-6).

c. When catalyst A is used, 10% acidity produces a much higher yield than does 15% acidity.

d. When catalyst B is used, 15% acidity produces a slightly higher yield than does 10% acidity.

The input variable levels that produce the maximum yield are catalyst B and 15% acidity.

Interval Plots

Interval plots are used to compare the averages of two or more variables, using any specified confidence interval. When intervals overlap, the averages of those variables being compared are considered to be equal. Figure 10-7 is an example of an interval plot, using a 95% confidence level. The plot shows that there is no significant difference in the average yield for acidity levels of 10% and 15%.

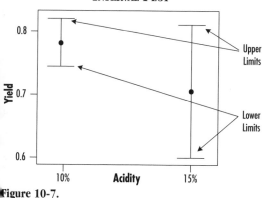

INTERVAL PLOT

Figure 10-7.

Example: Use an interval plot to determine if there is a significant difference in yield, based upon the type of catalyst used in the circuit board etching process.

Figure 10-8 indicates that there is a significant difference in average yield between catalyst A and B. Using catalyst B will result in greater average yields with less variation than will result when using catalyst A.

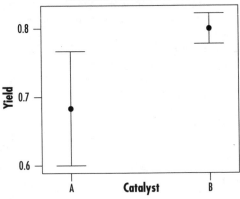

CATALYST INTERVAL PLOT

Figure 10-8.

Balanced ANOVA and General Linear Models (GLM)

Balanced ANOVA and GLM are general purpose tools that can be applied in a wide variety of circumstances. They are both used to analyze two or more variables that can be either

crossed or nested. Balanced ANOVA requires that all of the variables in the model have the same number of observations; i.e., the design must be balanced. With GLM, a balanced design is not required.

Example 1—Balanced ANOVA: Three blood samples were sent to four independent test laboratories for analysis of hemoglobin concentration. Each test was conducted twice with each of the samples. Table 10-9 shows the results of the tests. Is there a difference in the test results based on the location of the laboratories at a 0.05 significance level?

HEMOGLOBIN TEST RESULTS

Location	Sample	HgB Conc (gm/dl)
Ottawa	A	15.5
		14.4
	B	13.5
		13.6
	C	12.6
		13.7
Vancouver	A	14.3
		14.5
	B	16.6
		14.4
	C	13.4
		13.3

Table 10-9. (Continued on next page)

HEMOGLOBIN TEST RESULTS

Location	Sample	HgB Conc. (gm/dl)
Halifax	A	16.3
		18.4
	B	15.4
		17.3
	C	17.4
		18.5
Toronto	A	17.5
		16.5
	B	17.5
		16.5
	C	17.6
		18.5

Table 10-9. (Continued)

It appears that there is a statistically significant difference in the test results for average hemoglobin content, due to the location of the laboratory, since p is less than 0.05 (p=0.000). There is no evidence of a difference in the samples (p=0.721).

BALANCED ANOVA OUTPUT

ANOVA: HgB Conc. (gm/dl) versus Location, Sample			
Factor	Type	Levels	Values
Location	fixed	4	Halifax Ottawa Toronto Vancouver
Sample	fixed	3	A B C

Analysis of Variance for HgB Conc. (gm/dl)

Source	DF	SS	MS	F	P
Location	3	61.500	20.500	18.22	0.000
Sample	2	0.750	0.375	0.33	0.721
Error	18	20.250	1.125		
Total	23	82.500			

Table 10-10.

Example 2—GLM: A laminated wood products fabricator tested three factors (time, temperature, and adhesive) to determine how they affect average process yield. Table 10-11 shows a partial list of the test results.

A look at Table 10-12 suggests that time, temperature, and adhesive all have an impact on process yield, at a 0.05 significance level. Also, there appears to be an interaction effect between time and adhesive ($p = 0.048$).

The main effects plot for all three factors (Figure 10-9) shows that adhesive has the greatest main effect on yield, followed by temperature and time (time has the smallest main effect).

A look at the interaction plot for time and adhesive (Figure 10-10) shows an interaction effect. The greatest yield occurs when using the D100 adhesive and curing it for 15 minutes, which results in an average process yield of approximately 95%.

TEST RESULTS (PARTIAL LISTING)

Time	Temperature	Adhesive	Yield
10	20	D100	0.93
10	20	D100	0.91
10	20	D100	0.90
10	20	D100	0.96
—	—	—	—
—	—	—	—
—	—	—	—
15	25	D300	0.65
15	25	D300	0.62
15	25	D300	0.65
15	25	D300	0.67

Table 10-11.

GLM Output

General Linear Model: Yield versus Time, Temperature, Adhesive			
Factor	Type	Levels	Values
Time	fixed	2	10, 15
Temperature	fixed	2	20, 25
Adhesive	fixed	2	D100, D300

Analysis of Variance for Yield, Using Adjusted SS for Tests

Source	DF	Seq Ss	Adj SS	Adj MS	F	P
Time	1	0.008703	0.008703	0.008703	4.21	0.048
Temperature	1	0.085563	0.085563	0.085563	41.41	0.000
Adhesive	1	0.241803	0.241803	0.241803	117.03	0.000
Time x Temperature	1	0.000023	0.000023	0.000023	0.01	0.918
Temperature x Adhesive	1	0.001822	0.001822	0.001822	0.88	0.354
Time x Adhesive	11	0.008703	0.008703	0.008703	4.21	0.048
Error	33	0.068183	0.068183	0.002066		
Total	39	0.414798				

Table 10-12.

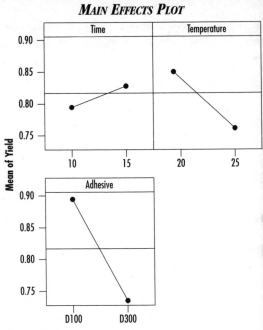

Figure 10-9.

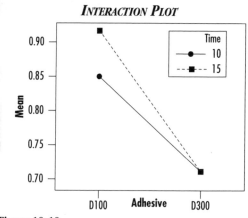

INTERACTION PLOT

Figure 10-10.

How to Perform Analysis of Variance (ANOVA)

1. Define test values for the null and alternate hypotheses.
2. Specify the significance level (α).
3. Determine the sample size and select a random sample or design a controlled experiment.
4. Select the appropriate ANOVA model (refer to the *Tool Selection Matrix*).
5. If conducting an experiment, run tests and collect data.
6. If $p < \alpha$, reject null hypothesis.
7. Use graphical tools to support your decisions and communicate results:

a. ANOM
b. Interval plots
c. Main effects plots
d. Interaction plots

APPENDIX A
References

Box, G.E.P,. Hunter, W.G., and Hunter, J.S. (1978), *Statistics for Experimenters: An Introduction to Design, Data Analysis, and Model Building,* John Wiley & Sons, New York.

Cox, D.R. (1958), *Planning of Experiments*, John Wiley & Sons, New York.

Evans, M., Hastings, N., and Peacock, B. (2000), *Statistical Distributions*, John Wiley & Sons, New York.

Hoerl, R. and Snee, R. (2002), *Statistical Thinking: Improving Business Performance*, Duxbury-Thomson Learning, Pacific Grove, CA.

Kachigan, S.K. (1991), *Multivariate Analysis: A Conceptual Introduction*, Radius Press, New York.

Lindsey, J.K. (1995), *Introductory Statistics: A Modelling Approach,* Oxford University Press, New York.

Montgomery, D.C. (1996), *Introduction To Statistical Quality Control*, John Wiley & Sons, New York.

Neter J., Kutner, M. H., Nachtsheim, C. J., and Wasserman,W. (1996), *Applied Linear Regression Models,* Richard D. Irwin, Inc., Burr Ridge, IL.

Rath & Strong (2002), *Six Sigma Pocket Guide*, Lexington, MA.

APPENDIX B
Glossary of Terms

Alpha Risk (α): the probability of committing a *Type I* error.

ANOVA: an approach that is used to compare the averages of two or more processes or factors; also used to identify the key drivers of variation among multiple process factors.

Beta Risk (β): the probability of committing a *Type II* error

Capability: the ability to produce products or services that consistently meet customer specifications.

Coefficient of Determination (r^2): a measure of how useful an x-variable (independent variable) is in predicting the value of the y-variable.

Common Cause Variation: variation that is inherent in a process and cannot be attributed to a single cause.

Confidence Interval: the range of values within which a population average or variance is expected to be contained.

Continuous Data: data that is the result of a measurement, e.g., distance, time, etc.

Continuous Distribution: a probability distribution consisting of continuous data, e.g., normal distribution.

Control Chart: a trend chart that provides insight into the center and spread of a distribution; frequently used to monitor and control processes.

Correlation Coefficient (r): a statistical measure of the relationship between two variables; values of r range from -1.00 to +1.00.

Discrete Data: data that is not the result of a measurement, e.g., counts, proportions, percentages, and attributes.

Discrete Distribution: a probability distribution consisting of a discrete data, e.g., binomial distribution.

Design of Experiments (DOE): a structured methodology that is used to improve process performance.

Gage R and R: used to access measurement system capability.

Hypothesis Test: used to confirm or disallow a theory about a specified population parameter.

Interaction Effect: the effect on the response variable that is produced by the combination of two or more input variables.

Main Effect: the effect on the response variable that is produced by changing the settings of a single input variable.

Multicollinearity: occurs when a regression model's input variables are strongly correlated.

Probability Distribution: a mathematical model that is used to describe the characteristics (shape, center, and spread) of a population.

Probability Plot: Graphical tool used to determine how well data fits a specific distribution. The normal probability plot is the one most commonly used.

Rational Subgroup: a sample where all items included in the sample were produced under very similar conditions.

Run Chart: used to plot a time series for a single variable.